CO-ASK-943

# Microsoft®
# Excel™ 2002

# MINUTE
# GUIDE

201 West 103rd Street
Indianapolis, IN 46290

**Joe Habraken**

# 10 Minute Guide to Microsoft® Excel™ 2002

## © 2002 by Que® Corporation

International Standard Book Number: 0-7897-2633-5

Library of Congress Catalog Card Number: 2001090286

Printed in the United States of America

First Printing: October 2001

04   03   02        8   7   6

## Trademarks

## Warning and Disclaimer

**Associate Publisher**
Greg Wiegand

**Acquisitions Editor**
Stephanie McComb

**Managing Editor**
Thomas F. Hayes

**Project Editor**
Tonya Simpson

**Indexer**
Mandie Frank

**Proofreader**
Plan-It Publishing

**Technical Editor**
Dallas Releford

**Team Coordinator**
Sharry Gregory

**Interior Designer**
Gary Adair

**Cover Designer**
Sandra Schroeder

**Page Layout**
Susan Geiselman

# Contents

# TABLE OF CONTENTS

# DEDICATION

*To my brother, Pete.*

# ACKNOWLEDGMENTS

Creating books like this takes a real team effort. I would like to thank Stephanie McComb, our acquisitions editor, who worked very hard to assemble the team that made this book a reality. Also, a tip of the hat and a thanks to Dallas Releford, who, as the technical editor for the project, did a fantastic job making sure that everything was correct and suggested a number of additions that made the book even more technically sound. Finally, a great big thanks to our project editor, Tonya Simpson, who ran the last leg of the race and made sure the book made it to press on time—what a great team of professionals.

# TELL US WHAT YOU THINK!

As the reader of this book, *you* are our most important critic and commentator. We value your opinion and want to know what we're doing right, what we could do better, what areas you'd like to see us publish in, and any other words of wisdom you're willing to pass our way.

As an associate publisher for Que, I welcome your comments. You can fax, e-mail, or write me directly to let me know what you did or didn't like about this book—as well as what we can do to make our books stronger.

*Please note that I cannot help you with technical problems related to the topic of this book, and that due to the high volume of mail I receive, I might not be able to reply to every message.*

When you write, please be sure to include this book's title and author, as well as your name and phone or fax number. I will carefully review your comments and share them with the author and editors who worked on the book.

Fax:       317-581-4666

E-mail:    feedback@quepublishing.com

Mail:      Greg Wiegand
           Que
           201 West 103rd Street
           Indianapolis, IN 46290 USA

# Introduction

Microsoft Excel 2002 is an incredibly versatile and easy-to-use spreadsheet program that can help you calculate and analyze numerical data for both large and small businesses. You can create simple spreadsheets, invoices, and even complex ledger reports. You even can save Excel data for use on the World Wide Web.

## THE WHAT AND WHY OF MICROSOFT EXCEL

Excel provides you with all the tools you need to quickly create many different types of business spreadsheets and reports. Whether you work at home or in a busy office, Microsoft Excel can help you do some heavy-duty number crunching. In Excel, you can

- Create spreadsheets that include formulas and built-in Excel functions
- Format numbers and text so that Excel printouts are easy to read
- Use clip art, pictures, borders, and colors to add interest to your spreadsheets
- Take Excel data and publish it to the World Wide Web

Additionally, Excel provides several features that make it easy for you to calculate the results of formulas and format your worksheets. You can

- Use the Excel Function Wizard to help you choose the right function to calculate the appropriate result.
- Use the Autoformat feature to quickly format an entire worksheet.
- Use the new speech feature for voice dictation and voice commands.

While providing you with many complex features, Microsoft Excel is easy to learn. This book will help you understand the possibilities awaiting you with Microsoft Excel 2002.

## WHY QUE'S *10 MINUTE GUIDE TO MICROSOFT EXCEL 2002*?

The *10 Minute Guide to Microsoft Excel 2002* can save you precious time while you get to know the different features in Microsoft Excel. Each lesson is designed to be completed in 10 minutes or less, so you'll be up to snuff on basic and advanced Excel skills quickly.

Although you can jump around between lessons, starting at the beginning is a good plan. The bare-bones basics are covered first, and more advanced topics are covered later. If you need help installing Excel, see the next section for instructions.

## INSTALLING EXCEL

You can install Microsoft Excel 2002 on a computer running Microsoft Windows 98, Windows NT 4.0, Windows 2000, or Windows XP. You can purchase Microsoft Excel as a standalone product on its own CD-ROM or as part of the Microsoft Office XP suite (which comes on a CD-ROM). Whether you are installing Excel as a standalone product or as part of the Microsoft Office XP suite, the installation steps are basically the same.

To install Excel, follow these steps:

1. Start your computer, and then insert the Excel 2002 or Microsoft XP Office CD in the CD-ROM drive. The CD-ROM should autostart, providing you with the opening installation screen (for either Excel or Office, depending on the CD with which you are working).

2. If the CD-ROM does not autostart, choose **Start, Run**. In the Run dialog box, type the letter of the CD-ROM drive, followed by **setup** (for example, **e:\setup**). If necessary, use the Browse button to locate and select the CD-ROM drive and the setup.exe program.

3. When the Setup Wizard prompts you, enter your name, organization, and CD key in the appropriate boxes.

4. Choose **Next** to continue.

5. The next wizard screen provides instructions to finish the installation. Complete the installation. Select **Next** to advance from screen to screen after providing the appropriate information requested by the wizard.

After you finish the installation from the CD, icons for Excel and any other Office applications you have installed will appear on the Windows Start menu. Lesson 2 in this book provides you with a step-by-step guide to starting Excel 2002.

## CONVENTIONS USED IN THIS BOOK

To help you move through the lessons easily, commands, options, and icons you need to select, and keys you need to press appear in **bold** type.

In telling you to choose menu commands, this book uses the format *menu title, menu command*. For example, the statement "Choose **File, Properties**" means to open the File menu and select the Properties command.

In addition to those conventions, the *10 Minute Guide to Microsoft Excel 2002* uses the following sidebars to identify helpful information:

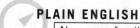

**PLAIN ENGLISH**

New or unfamiliar terms are defined in term sidebars.

**TIP**

Read these tips for ideas that cut corners and confusion.

**CAUTION**

This icon identifies areas where new users often run into trouble. These sidebars offer practical solutions to those problems.

# LESSON 1
# What's New in Excel 2002

*This lesson introduces you to Microsoft Access, and you learn what's new in Access 2002.*

## INTRODUCING EXCEL 2002

Excel is a powerful spreadsheet program that can help you create worksheets and invoices and do both simple and sophisticated number crunching. It is designed to help you calculate the results of formulas and help you analyze numerical data. Excel also makes it easy for you to take numerical information and display the data in a variety of chart types. You even can add graphics and other objects to your Excel worksheets to create professional-looking printouts and business reports.

Excel provides several user-friendly features that make it easy for you to get your data into a worksheet and format the information. Excel also makes it easy for you to do calculations, whether you use formulas that you create or use any of the numerous functions (built-in formulas) that Excel provides. There are financial, statistical, logical, and even engineering functions (Excel functions are covered in Lesson 6, "Performing Calculations with Functions").

The following are some of the Excel features with which you will become familiar in this book:

- **Excel templates**—Excel provides several templates—such as a time card, expense sheet, and sales invoice—that provide you with a ready-made worksheet containing formulas and formatting. All you have to do is enter the appropriate information to create a complete worksheet. Excel templates are discussed in the next lesson.

- **Fill feature**—The Fill feature enables you to add series of numbers or quickly copy information from one cell to several cells. The Fill feature is discussed in Lesson 3.

- **Wizards**—Wizards help you use many Excel features. They guide you through a number of Excel processes, including the creation of functions (covered in Lesson 6) and the insertion of charts into a worksheet (charts are discussed in Lessons 17 and 18).

**PLAIN ENGLISH**

> **Wizard**    A feature that guides you step by step through a particular process in Excel, such as creating a new chart.

## WHAT'S NEW IN EXCEL 2002

Excel 2002 is similar in look and feel to Excel 2000, the previous version of this powerful spreadsheet software. Excel 2002 provides the same adaptive menu and toolbar system found in Excel 2000 that customizes the commands and icons listed on your menus and toolbars based on the commands you use most frequently.

Excel 2002 also includes several new features, such as task panes and voice dictation, that make it even easier for you to create and maintain your Excel workbooks. Let's take a look at some of the important changes to the Excel 2002 software.

## INTRODUCING TASK PANES

One of the biggest changes to the Excel environment (and all the Microsoft Office XP suite applications, such as Word 2002, Access 2002, and PowerPoint 2002) is the introduction of the Office task pane. The task pane is a special pane that appears on the right side of the Excel application window when you use certain Excel features (features that formerly were controlled using dialog boxes).

For example, when you start a new Excel workbook, the New Workbook task pane appears (see Figure 1.1). This task pane makes it easy for you to start a new blank workbook or create a workbook using one of the spreadsheet templates provided by Excel.

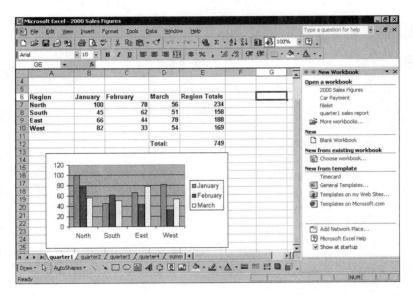

**FIGURE 1.1**
*The New Workbook task pane makes it easy for you to create a new Excel workbook.*

Other task panes that you will run across as you work in Excel are the Office Clipboard and the Clip Gallery. The Office Clipboard enables you to copy or cut multiple items from an Excel workbook and then paste them into new locations. The Clip Gallery enables you to insert clip art and other images into your Excel worksheets. Task panes are discussed in this book, when appropriate, as you explore the various Excel features.

## INTRODUCING VOICE DICTATION AND VOICE COMMANDS

One of the most exciting new features in Excel 2002 (and the entire Office XP suite) is voice dictation and voice-activated commands. If your computer is outfitted with a sound card, speakers, and a microphone (or a microphone with an earphone headset), you can dictate information into your Excel worksheets. You also can use voice commands to activate the menu system and toolbars in Excel.

Before you can really take advantage of the Speech feature, you must train it so that it can easily recognize your speech patterns and intonation. After the Speech feature is trained, you can effectively use it to dictate text entries or access various application commands without using a keyboard or mouse.

**CAUTION**

> **Requirements for Getting the Most Out of the Speech Feature**   To make the Speech feature useful, you will need a fairly high-quality microphone. Microsoft suggests a microphone/headset combination. The Speech feature also requires a more powerful computer. Microsoft suggests using a computer with 128MB of RAM and a Pentium II (or later) processor running at a minimum of 400MHz. A computer that meets or exceeds these higher standards should be capable of getting the most out of the Speech feature.

If you are new to Excel, you might want to explore the other lessons in this book before you attempt to use the Speech feature. Having a good understanding of how Excel operates and the features that it provides will allow you to get the most out of the Speech feature.

## TRAINING THE SPEECH FEATURE

The first time you start the Speech feature in Excel, you are required to configure and train the feature. Follow these steps to get the Speech feature up and running:

1. In Excel, select the **Tools** menu, point at **Speech,** and then select **Speech Recognition**. The Welcome to Office Speech Recognition dialog box appears. To begin the process of setting up your microphone and training the Speech feature, click the **Next** button.

2. The first screen of the Microphone Wizard appears. It asks you to be sure your microphone and speakers are connected to your computer. If you have a headset microphone, this screen shows you how to adjust the microphone for use. Click **Next** to continue.

3. The next wizard screen asks you to read a short text passage so that your microphone volume level can be adjusted (see Figure 1.2). When you have finished reading the text, click **Next** to continue.

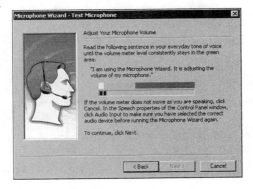

**FIGURE 1.2**
*The Microphone Wizard adjusts the volume of your microphone.*

4. On the next screen, you are told that if you have a headset microphone, you can click **Finish** and proceed to the speech recognition training. If you have a different type of microphone, you are asked to read another text passage. The text then is played back to you. This is to determine whether the microphone is placed at an appropriate distance from your mouth. When you get a satisfactory playback, click **Finish**.

When you finish working with the Microphone Wizard, the Voice
Training Wizard appears. This wizard collects samples of your speech
and, in essence, educates the Speech feature as to how you speak.

To complete the voice training process, follow these steps:

1. After reading the information on the opening screen, click
   **Next** to begin the voice training process.

2. On the next screen, you are asked to provide your gender and
   age (see Figure 1.3). After specifying the correct information,
   click **Next**.

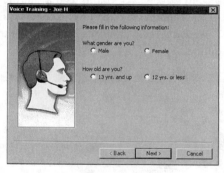

**FIGURE 1.3**
*Supply the voice trainer with your gender and age.*

3. On the next wizard screen, you see an overview of how the
   voice training will proceed. You also see directions for how
   to pause the training session. Click **Next**.

4. The next wizard screen reminds you to adjust your microphone. You also are reminded that you need a quiet room
   when training the Speech feature. When you are ready to
   begin training the speech recognition feature, click **Next**.

5. On the next screen, you are asked to read some text. Each
   word is highlighted as the wizard recognizes it. After finish-
   ing with this screen, continue by clicking **Next**.

**6.** You are asked to read text on several subsequent screens. Words are selected as the wizard recognizes them.

**7.** When you complete the training screens, your profile is updated. Click **Finish** on the wizard's final screen.

You now are ready to use the Speech feature. Using the Voice Dictation and Voice Command features are discussed in Lesson 3, "Entering Data into the Worksheet."

 **CAUTION**

> **The Speech Feature Works Better Over Time**    Be advised that the voice feature's performance improves as you use it. As you learn to pronounce your words more carefully, the Speech feature tunes itself to your speech patterns. You might need to do additional training sessions to fine-tune the Speech feature.

This lesson introduced you to Excel 2002 and some of the new available features, such as task panes and the Speech feature. In the next lesson, you will learn how to start Excel and create a new workbook.

# LESSON 2
# Creating a New Workbook

*In this lesson, you learn how to start and exit Excel and you become familiar with the Excel window. You also learn how to create new workbooks and open existing workbook files.*

## STARTING EXCEL

Excel provides you with all the tools you need to create both simple and complex spreadsheets. You also will find that Excel is a fairly typical Windows program and provides you with all the features, such as menu bars and toolbars, with which you are familiar from working in the Windows environment.

To start Excel from the Windows desktop, follow these steps:

1. Click the **Start** button, and the Start menu appears.

2. Choose **Programs**, and the Programs menu appears.

3. Choose **Microsoft Excel** to start the program.

## UNDERSTANDING THE EXCEL WINDOW

When you click the Microsoft Excel icon, the Excel application window appears, displaying a blank workbook labeled Book1 (see Figure 2.1). On the right side of the Excel window is the New Workbook task pane. This task pane enables you to open existing Excel workbooks or create new blank workbooks or workbooks based on various Excel templates (which is discussed later in the lesson).

**TIP**

> **Close the Task Pane**   If you would like a little more room to work on the current workbook sheet in the Excel window, click the **Close** (**x**) button on the task pane.

When you work in Excel, you use workbook files to hold your numerical data, formulas, and other objects, such as Excel charts. Each Excel workbook can consist of several sheets; each sheet is called a worksheet.

**PLAIN ENGLISH**

> **Workbook**   An Excel file is called a workbook. Each workbook consists of several worksheets made up of rows and columns of information.

You enter your numbers and formulas on one of the workbook's worksheets. Each worksheet consists of 256 columns. The columns begin with A and proceed through the alphabet. The 27th column is AA, followed by AB, AC, and this convention for naming subsequent columns continues through the entire alphabet until you end up with the last column (column 256), which is designated IV.

Each worksheet also consists of 65,536 rows. The intersection of a column and a row on the worksheet is called a cell. Each cell has an address that consists of the column and row that intersect to make the cell. For example, the very first cell on a worksheet is in column A and row 1, so the cell's address is A1.

**PLAIN ENGLISH**

> **Worksheet**   One sheet in an Excel workbook. Each worksheet consists of 256 columns and 65,536 rows (plenty of space to create even the most enormous spreadsheet).

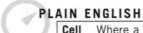

**PLAIN ENGLISH**

> **Cell**    Where a row and column intersect, each cell has
> an address that consists of the column letter and row
> number (A1, B3, C4, and so on). You enter data and for-
> mulas in the cells to create your worksheets.

Figure 2.1 shows cell A1 highlighted in worksheet 1 (designated as
Sheet1 on its tab) of Workbook 1 (designated in the title bar as Book1;
this will change to a particular filename after you name the workbook
using the Save function).

**FIGURE 2.1**

*Excel provides a new workbook and the menus and toolbars necessary for doing
some serious number crunching.*

The Excel window shown here includes many of the various elements available in other Office applications, such as Word or PowerPoint. These elements include a menu bar (from which you select commands), a status bar (which displays the status of the current activity), and toolbars (which contain buttons and drop-down lists that provide quick access to various commands and features).

In addition, the window contains several elements that are unique to Excel, as shown in Table 2.1.

**Table 2.1**    Elements of the Excel Window

| Element | Description |
| --- | --- |
| Formula bar | When you enter information into a cell, it appears in the Formula bar. You can use the Formula bar to edit the data later. The cell's location also appears in the Formula bar. |
| Column headings | The letters across the top of the worksheet, which identify the columns in the worksheet. |
| Row headings | The numbers down the side of the worksheet, which identify the rows in the worksheet. |
| Cell selector | The dark outline that indicates the active cell. (It highlights the cell in which you are currently working.) |
| Worksheet tabs | These tabs help you move from worksheet to worksheet within the workbook. |

## STARTING A NEW WORKBOOK

As you've already seen, when you start Excel, it opens a new blank workbook. It is ready to accept data entry, which is discussed in Lesson 3, "Entering Data into the Worksheet."

The empty workbook that appears when you start Excel is pretty much a blank canvas, but Excel also enables you to create new workbooks based on a template. A *template* is a predesigned workbook that you can modify to suit your needs. Excel contains templates for creating invoices, expense reports, and other common business accounting forms.

To create a new workbook, follow these steps:

1. Open the **File** menu and select **New**. The New Workbook task pane appears on the right side of the Excel window (if you did not close it as outlined earlier, it should already be open).

2. The New Workbook task pane enables you to create new blank workbooks or create workbooks based on a template (see Figure 2.2).

**FIGURE 2.2**
*The New Workbook task pane provides quick access to commands for creating new Excel workbooks.*

3. To create a blank workbook, click the **Blank Workbook** icon. A new blank workbook opens in the Excel window.

 **PLAIN ENGLISH**

**Instant Workbook** You also can quickly start a new blank workbook by clicking the **New** button on the Standard toolbar.

Blank templates are fine when you have a design in mind for the overall look of the workbook. However, for some help with workbook layout and formatting, you can base your new workbook on an Excel template. To use an Excel template, follow these steps:

1. Click the **General Templates** icon in the New from Template menu of the New Workbook task pane. The Templates dialog box appears.

2. Click the **Spreadsheet Solutions** tab on the Templates dialog box. The various workbook template icons appear (see Figure 2.3).

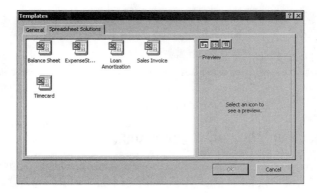

**FIGURE 2.3**
*The Spreadsheet Solutions tab provides the different Excel templates.*

3. Select a template by clicking its icon, and then click **OK** or press **Enter**. A new workbook opens onscreen with a default name based on the template you chose. For example, if you

chose the Timecard template, the new workbook is named
Timecard1, as shown at the top of Figure 2.4.

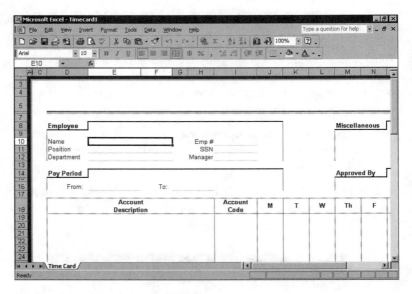

**FIGURE 2.4**
*A new workbook based on a template provides a basic layout for a particular*
*business form.*

## SAVING AND NAMING A WORKBOOK

Whether you build your workbook from a blank template or use one
of the Excel templates, after you enter some data into the workbook,
you should save the file (you learn about data entry in Lesson 3,
"Entering Data into the Worksheet"). Also, because changes that you
make to the workbook are not automatically saved, you should occasionally save the edited version of your work.

The first time you save a workbook, you must name it and specify a
location where it should be saved. Follow these steps to save your
workbook:

1. Open the **File** menu and select **Save**, or click the **Save** button on the Standard toolbar. The Save As dialog box appears (see Figure 2.5).

**FIGURE 2.5**
*Specify the name and location for your new workbook in the Save As dialog box.*

2. Type the name you want to give the workbook in the **File Name** text box. You can use up to 218 characters, including any combination of letters, numbers, and spaces.

3. Normally, Excel saves your workbooks in the My Documents folder. To save the file to a different folder or drive (such as a network drive), select a new location using the **Save In** list.

**CAUTION**

**The Folder I Want to Save In Doesn't Exist!**   You can create a new folder from the Save As dialog box: Click the **Create New Folder** button on the toolbar of the Save As dialog box, type a name for the new folder, and then press **Enter**.

4. Click **Save** to save your workbook and close the Save As dialog box.

To save changes that you make to a workbook you previously saved, just click the **Save** button on the Standard toolbar. You also can press the shortcut key combination of **Ctrl+S** to save changes to your workbook.

## SAVING A WORKBOOK UNDER A NEW NAME OR LOCATION

There might be an occasion when you want to save a copy of a particular workbook under a different name or in a different location. Excel makes it easy for you to make duplicates of a workbook. Follow these steps:

1. Select the **File** menu and select **Save As**. The Save As dialog box opens, just as if you were saving the workbook for the first time.

2. To save the workbook under a new name, type the new filename over the existing name in the **File Name** text box.

3. To save the new file on a different drive or in a different folder, select the drive letter or the folder from the **Save In** list.

4. To save the new file in a different format (such as Lotus 1-2-3 or Quattro Pro), click the **Save As Type** drop-down arrow and select the desired format.

5. Click the **Save** button or press **Enter**.

**TIP**

---
**Saving Excel Workbooks in Other File Formats**
Occasionally, you might share Excel workbook data with co-workers or colleagues who don't use Excel. Being able to save Excel workbooks in other file formats, such as Lotus 1-2-3 (as discussed in step 4), enables you to provide another user a file that they can open in their spreadsheet program.

---

## OPENING AN EXISTING WORKBOOK

If you have a workbook you've previously saved that you would like to work on, you must open the file first, before you can make any changes. Follow these steps to open an existing workbook:

1. Open the **File** menu and select **Open**, or click the **Open** button on the Standard toolbar. The Open dialog box shown in Figure 2.6 appears.

**FIGURE 2.6**
*Use the Open dialog box to locate and open an existing Excel workbook.*

2. If the file is not located in the current folder, open the **Look In** drop-down list box and select the correct drive and folder.

3. Select the file you want to open in the files and folders list.

4. To see a preview of the workbook before you open it, click the **Views** button and select **Preview**. Excel displays the contents of the workbook in a window to the right of the dialog box.

5. Click **Open** to open the currently selected workbook.

**TIP**

> **Recently Used Workbooks**    If the workbook you want to open is one of your four most recently used workbooks, you'll find it listed at the bottom of the File menu. It also will be listed at the top of the New Workbook task pane (if the task pane is active).

## CLOSING WORKBOOKS

When you have finished with a particular workbook and want to continue working in Excel, you easily can close the current workbook. Click the **Close** (x) button in the upper-right corner of the workbook. (There are two Close buttons: The one on top closes Excel; the one below it closes the current workbook window.) You also can close the current workbook by selecting **File**, **Close**. If you have changed the workbook since the last time you saved it, you will be prompted to save any changes.

**TIP**

> **It's Closing Time!**    If you have more than one workbook open, you can close all of them at once by holding down the **Shift** key, selecting the **File** menu, and then selecting **Close All**.

## EXITING EXCEL

When you have finished working with Excel, you need to exit the application. This closes all workbooks that are currently open. To exit Excel, select the **File** menu and select **Exit**. Or, you can click the **Close** (x) button at the upper-right corner of the Excel window.

If you have changed any of the workbooks with which you were working, you are prompted to save changes to these workbook files before exiting Excel.

In this lesson, you learned how to start and exit Excel. You also learned how to open a new workbook and create a workbook on an Excel template. Finally, you were provided the ins and outs of opening and closing Excel workbooks. In the next lesson, you will learn how to enter different kinds of data into Excel when you build a workbook file.

# LESSON 3
# Entering Data into the Worksheet

*In this lesson, you learn how to enter different data types into an Excel worksheet and use special features, such as AutoComplete and the Speech feature.*

## UNDERSTANDING EXCEL DATA TYPES

When you work in Excel, you enter different types of information, such as text, numbers, dates, times, formulas, and functions (which is a special built-in formula provided by Excel). Excel data basically comes in two varieties: labels and values.

A label is a text entry; it is called a label because it typically provides descriptive information, such as the name of a person, place, or thing. A label has no numerical significance in Excel; it's just there to describe accompanying values.

**PLAIN ENGLISH**

**Label**   Any text entry made on an Excel worksheet.

A value is data that has numerical significance. This includes numbers, dates, and times that you enter on your worksheet. Values can be acted on by formulas and functions. Formulas are discussed in Lesson 4, "Performing Simple Calculations," and Excel functions are discussed in Lesson 6, "Performing Calculations with Functions."

## ENTERING TEXT

Text is any combination of letters, numbers, and spaces. By default,
text is automatically left-aligned in a cell, whereas numerical data is
right-aligned.

To enter text into a cell, follow these steps:

1. Use your mouse or the keyboard arrows to select the cell in
   which you want to enter text.

2. Type the text. As you type, your text appears in the cell and
   in the Formula bar, as shown in Figure 3.1.

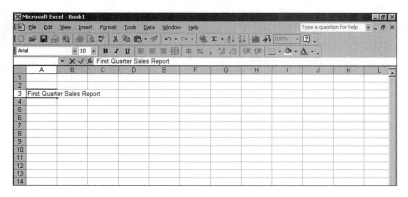

**FIGURE 3.1**
*Data that you enter into a cell also appears in the Formula bar as you type it.*

3. Press **Enter**. Your text appears in the cell, left-aligned. The
   cell selector moves down one cell. You also can press **Tab** or
   an arrow key to enter the text and move to the next cell to the
   right (or in the direction of the arrow).

**CAUTION**

> **But My Entry Doesn't Fit!**   When text does not fit into a cell (because of the column width set for that column), Excel displays the information in one of two ways: If the next cell is empty, the text overflows into that cell, allowing you to see your entire entry. If the cell to the right of your entry is not empty, you will be able to see only the portion of your entry that fits within the confines of the cell. This can easily be remedied by changing the column width. You'll learn about changing column widths in Lesson 14, "Inserting and Removing Cells, Rows, and Columns."

**TIP**

> **Entering Numbers As Text**   To enter a number that you want treated as text (such as a ZIP code), precede the entry with a single quotation mark ('), as in '46220. The single quotation mark is an alignment prefix that tells Excel to treat the following characters as text and left-align them in the cell. You do not have to do this to "text" numerical entries, but it ensures that they will not be mistakenly acted upon by formulas or functions.

## TIPS ON ENTERING COLUMN AND ROW LABELS

Column and row labels identify your data. Column labels appear across the top of the worksheet beneath the worksheet title (if any). Row labels are entered on the left side of the worksheet.

Column labels describe what the numbers in a column represent. Typically, column labels specify time intervals such as years, months, days, quarters, and so on. Row labels describe what the numbers in each row represent. Typically, row labels specify data categories, such as product names, employee names, or income and expense items in a budget.

When entering your column labels, enter the first label and press the **Tab** key instead of pressing Enter. This moves you to the next cell on the right so that you can enter another column label. When entering row labels, use the down-arrow key instead of the Tab key. Figure 3.2 shows the various labels for a quarterly sales summary.

Column headings

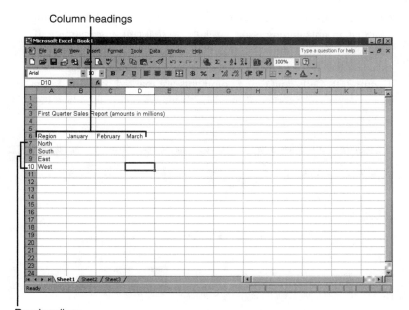

Row headings

**FIGURE 3.2**
*Column and row headings serve as labels for the data you enter on the work-sheet.*

If you need to enter similar data (such as a series of months or years) as column or row labels, you can enter them quickly as a series; this technique is discussed later in this lesson.

## ADDING COMMENTS TO CELLS

Although not really considered cell content (such as labels and values), you can add comments to particular cells. These comments allow you to associate information with a cell—information that does not appear (by default) with the worksheet when sent to the printer.

Comments are similar to placing a Post-it note on a cell, reminding you that an outstanding issue is related to that cell. For example, if you need to check the value that you've placed in a particular cell to make sure that it's accurate, you can place a comment in the cell (see Figure 3.3). Cells containing comments are marked with a red triangle in the upper-right corner of the cell. To view a comment, place the mouse pointer on the comment triangle.

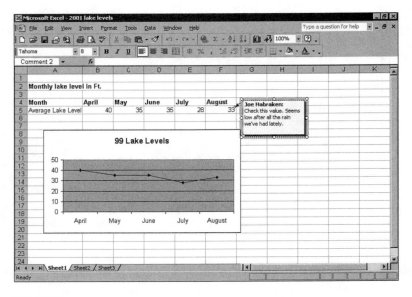

**FIGURE 3.3**
*Comments can be added to cells as a kind of electronic Post-it note.*

To insert a comment into a cell, follow these steps:

1. Click the cell in which you want to place the comment.

2. Select **Insert**, **Comment**. A comment box appears next to the cell.

3. Type your information into the comment box.

4. Click anywhere else in the worksheet to close the comment box.

You also can easily remove comments from cells. Select the cell, and then select **Edit** and point at **Clear**. On the cascading menu, select **Comments** to remove the comment.

## ENTERING NUMBERS

Data that serves as the values in your workbooks can include the numeric characters 0–9. Because formulas also are considered values (you learn about simple calculations in Lesson 4, "Performing Simple Calculations"), other valid value characters include symbols such as +, – , /, and *. You also can use characters such as a comma (,), a percent sign (%), or a dollar sign ($) in your values. You will find, however, that you can save yourself a few data-entry keystrokes and add these characters using different Excel formatting options (you learn about Excel formatting in Lesson 11, "Changing How Numbers and Text Look").

For example, you could enter the dollar amount $700.00 including the dollar sign and the decimal point. However, it's probably faster to enter 700 into the cell and then format all the cells that contain dollar amounts after you have entered all the data.

To enter a value, follow these steps:

1. Click in the cell where you want to enter the value.

2. Type the value. To enter a negative number, precede it with a minus sign or surround it with parentheses.

3. Press **Enter** or the **Tab** key; the value appears in the cell right-aligned. Figure 3.4 shows various values entered into a simple worksheet.

|    | A | B | C | D | E | F |
|----|---|---|---|---|---|---|
| 1  |   |   |   |   |   |   |
| 2  |   |   |   |   |   |   |
| 3  | First Quarter Sales Report (amounts in millions) |   |   |   |   |   |
| 4  |   |   |   |   |   |   |
| 5  |   |   |   |   |   |   |
| 6  | Region | January | February | March |   |   |
| 7  | North | 70 | 35 | 90 |   |   |
| 8  | South | 100 | 56 | 66 |   |   |
| 9  | East | 54 | 84 | 55 |   |   |
| 10 | West | 66 | 33 | 70 |   |   |
| 11 |   |   |   |   |   |   |
| 12 |   |   |   |   |   |   |
| 13 |   |   |   |   |   |   |
| 14 |   |   |   |   |   |   |

**FIGURE 3.4**
*Values are right-aligned in a cell.*

**TIP**

**What Are All Those Pound Signs?**    If you enter a number and it appears in the cell as all pound signs (#######) or in scientific notation (such as 7.78E+06), the cell just isn't wide enough to display the entire number. To fix it, double-click the right border of the column's heading. The column expands to fit the largest entry in that column. See Lesson 14, "Inserting and Removing Cells, Rows, and Columns," for more information on working with column widths.

## ENTERING DATES AND TIMES

Dates that you enter into an Excel workbook have numerical significance. Excel converts the date into a number that reflects the number of days that have elapsed since January 1, 1900. Even though you won't see this number (Excel displays your entry as a normal date), the number is used whenever you use this date in a calculation. Times also are considered values. Excel sees them as the number of seconds that have passed since 12 a.m.

Follow these steps to enter a date or time:

1. Click in the cell where you want to enter a date or a time.

2. To enter a date, use the format MM/DD/YY or the format MM-DD-YY, as in 5/9/01 or 5-9-01.

   To enter a time, be sure to specify a.m. or p.m., as in 7:21 p or 8:22 a.

**TIP**

> **A.M. or P.M.?**    Unless you type am or pm after your time entry, Excel assumes that you are using a 24-hour international clock. Therefore, 8:20 is assumed to be a.m., not p.m. (20:20 would be p.m.: 8 plus 12 hours). Therefore, if you mean p.m., type the entry as 8:20 pm (or 8:20 p). Note that you must type a space between the time and the am or pm notation.

3. Press **Enter**. As long as Excel recognizes the entry as a date or a time, it appears right-aligned in the cell. If Excel doesn't recognize it, it's treated as text and left-aligned.

After you enter your date or time, you can format the cells to display the date or time exactly as you want it to appear, such as September 16, 1998, or 16:50 (international time). If you're entering a column of dates or times, you can format the entire column in one easy step. To format a column, click the column header to select the column. Then open the **Format** menu and select **Cells**. On the **Numbers** tab, select the date or time format you want to use (you learn more about formatting text and numbers in Lesson 11).

## COPYING (FILLING) THE SAME DATA TO OTHER CELLS

Another way to enter labels or values onto a sheet is to use the Fill feature. You can copy (fill) an entry into surrounding cells. For example, suppose you have a list of salespeople on a worksheet, and they will each get a $100 bonus. You can enter the 100 once and then use the Fill feature to insert multiple copies of 100 into nearby cells. To use the Fill feature for copying, follow these steps:

1. Click the fill handle of the cell (the small block in the lower-right corner of the cell) that holds the data that you want to copy (see Figure 3.5).

2. Drag the fill handle down or to the right to copy the data to adjacent cells. A data tag appears to let you know exactly what data is being copied into the cells.

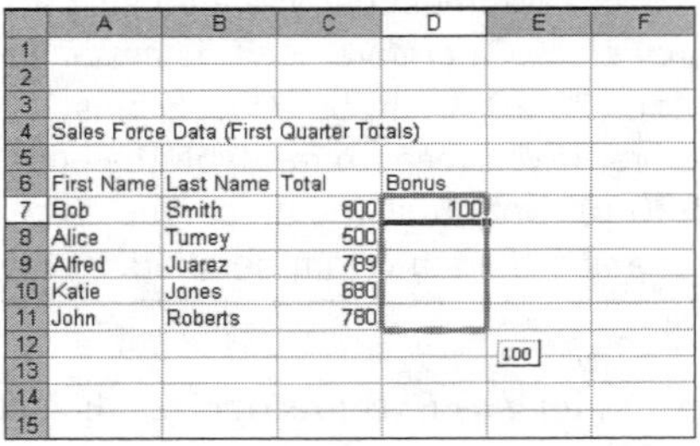

**FIGURE 3.5**
*Drag the fill handle to copy the contents of a cell into neighboring cells.*

3. Release the mouse button. The data is "filled" into the selected cells.

When you release the mouse, a shortcut box for Fill options appears at the end of the cells that you filled. Copy Cells is the default option for the Fill feature, so you can ignore the shortcut box for the moment. It does come into play when you enter a series in the next section.

**CAUTION**

**Watch That Fill!** The data you're copying replaces any existing data in the adjacent cells that you fill.

## Entering a Series of Numbers, Dates, and Other Data

Entering a value *series* (such as January, February, and March or 1, 2, 3, 4, and so on) is accomplished using the Fill feature discussed in the preceding section. When you use the Fill feature, Excel looks at the cell holding the data and tries to determine whether you want to just copy that information into the adjacent cells or use it as the starting point for a particular series of data. For example, with Monday entered in the first cell of the series, Excel automatically inserts Tuesday, Wednesday, and so on into the adjacent cells when you use the Fill feature.

Sometimes, Excel isn't quite sure whether you want to copy the data when you use Fill or create a series. This is where the Fill options shortcut box comes in. It enables you to select how the Fill feature should treat the data that you have "filled" into the adjacent cells. Figure 3.6 shows the creation of a day series using Fill.

**FIGURE 3.6**
*Fill also can be used to create a series of data in adjacent cells.*

When you create a series using Fill, the series progresses by one increment. For example, a series starting with 1 would proceed to 2, 3, 4, and so on. If you want to create a series that uses some increment other than 1, you must create a custom series, which is discussed in the next section.

## ENTERING A CUSTOM SERIES

If you want to create a series such as 10, 20, 30, where the series uses a custom increment between the values, you need to create a custom series. Excel provides two ways to create a custom series. To create a custom series using Fill, follow these steps:

1. Enter the first value of the series into a cell.

2. Enter the second value in the series into the next cell. For example, you might enter **10** into the first cell and then **20** into the second cell. This lets Excel know that the increment for the series is 10.

3. Select both cells by clicking the first cell and dragging over the second cell.

4. Drag the fill handle of the second cell to the other cells that will be part of the series. Excel analyzes the two cells, sees the incremental pattern, and re-creates it in subsequent cells.

You also can create a custom series using the Series dialog box. This enables you to specify the increment or step value for the series and even specify a stop value for the series.

1. Enter the first value of the series into a cell.

2. Select the cells that you want included in the series.

3. Select the **Edit** menu, point at **Fill**, and then select **Series**. The Series dialog box opens (see Figure 3.7).

**FIGURE 3.7**
*The Series dialog box enables you to create a custom series.*

4. Enter the Step Value for the series. You also can enter a Stop Value for the series if you did not select the cells used for the series in step 2. For example, if you want to add a series to a column of cells and have clicked in the first cell that will receive a value, using a Stop Value (such as 100 for a series that will go from 1 to 100) will "stop" entering values in the cells when it reaches 100—the Stop Value.

5. Click **OK** to create the series.

**TIP**

**Different Series Types**    Not only can you create a linear series using the Series dialog box (as discussed in the steps in this section), but you also can create growth and date series. In a growth series, the data you're copying replaces any existing data in the adjacent cells that you fill.

## TAKING ADVANTAGE OF AUTOCOMPLETE

Another useful feature that Excel provides to help take some of the drudgery out of entering information into a workbook is the AutoComplete feature. Excel keeps a list of all the labels that you enter on a worksheet by column. For example, suppose you have a worksheet tracking sales in Europe and you are entering country names, such as Germany, Italy, and so on, multiple times into a particular column in the worksheet. After you enter Germany the first time, it becomes part of the AutoComplete list for that column. The next time you enter the letter G into a cell in that column, Excel completes the entry as "Germany."

You also can select an entry from the AutoComplete list. This allows you to see the entire list of available entries. Follow these steps:

1. Enter your text and value data as needed onto the worksheet.

2. If you want to select a text entry from the AutoComplete list to fill an empty cell, right-click that cell. A shortcut menu appears.

3. Select **Pick from List** from the shortcut menu. A list of text entries (in alphabetical order) appears below the current cell.

4. Click a word in the list to insert it into the current, empty cell.

**TIP**

> **Adding Data to Excel Using Voice Recognition**    The Office Speech Recognition feature also can be used to enter data into an Excel worksheet and to perform voice commands. If you have a computer that is set up with a sound card and microphone, you can use this feature. See Lesson 1, "What's New in Excel 2002," for more information on setting up the voice feature in Excel.

## DICTATING WORKSHEET INFORMATION

If you have a microphone and have set up the Speech Recognition feature as discussed in Lesson 1, you also can dictate information into an Excel workbook. You can dictate both labels and values into the worksheet cells.

To dictate entries into an Excel worksheet, follow these steps:

1. To turn on voice dictation, select **Tools**, point at **Speech**, and then select **Speech Recognition**. The Language bar appears in the Excel window with the Dictation feature turned on (see Figure 3.8).

2. Dictate the contents of the cell. Use the Enter key or the arrow keys to move to the next cell you want to fill.

3. Dictate the contents of other cells as required.

4. To turn off the Dictation mode, click the **Microphone** on the Language bar.

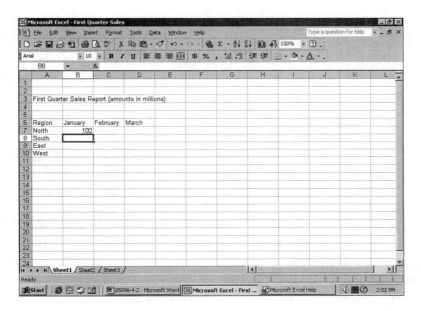

**FIGURE 3.8**
*The Office Voice Recognition feature allows you to dictate information into a worksheet.*

Dictating numerical values into a cell is a little trickier than dictating a text label. Numbers less than 20 are spelled as words in Excel. To force these values to be entered as actual numbers, say "force num," pause for a second, and then say the number, such as "6."

**TIP**

> **Turn on Dictation with a Voice Command**  If the Language bar is already present in the Excel workspace, you can say "dictation" to turn on the feature.

You also can use the Speech feature to issue voice commands. You can open and select menus in Excel and even navigate dialog boxes using voice commands.

To use voice commands, open the Language bar (click **Tools,** **Speech**). Click the **Microphone** icon, if necessary, to expand the Language bar. Then, click the **Voice Command** icon on the bar (or say "voice command").

To open a particular menu, such as the Format menu, say "format." Then, to open a particular submenu such as Font, say "font." In the case of these voice commands, the Font dialog box opens.

You then can navigate a particular dialog box using voice commands. In the Font dialog box, for example, to change the size of the font, say "size"; this activates the Size box that controls font size. Then, say the size of the font, such as "14." You also can activate other font attributes in the dialog box in this manner. Say the name of the area of the dialog box you want to use, and then say the name of the feature you want to turn on or select.

When you have finished working with a particular dialog box, say "OK" (or "Cancel" or "Apply," as needed). The dialog box closes and provides you with the features you selected in the dialog box. When you have finished using voice commands, say "microphone," or click the **Microphone** icon on the Language bar.

You also can activate buttons on the various toolbars using voice commands. For example, you could sort an Excel worksheet by a particular column by clicking in the column and then saying "sort ascending." The Sort Ascending button on the Excel toolbar becomes active and your data is sorted.

In this lesson, you learned how to enter different types of data and how to automate data entry with features such as AutoComplete and the Speech feature. In the next lesson, you learn how to perform simple calculations in a workbook.

# LESSON 4
# Performing Simple Calculations

*In this lesson, you learn how to use formulas to calculate results in your worksheets.*

## UNDERSTANDING EXCEL FORMULAS

One way to add calculations to an Excel workbook is to create your own formulas. Formulas typically are used to perform calculations such as addition, subtraction, multiplication, and division. More complex calculations are better left to Excel Functions, which is a built-in set of formulas that provide financial, mathematical, and statistical calculations. You learn more about functions in Lesson 6, "Performing Calculations with Functions."

Formulas that you create typically include cell addresses that reference cells on which you want to perform a calculation. Formulas also consist of mathematical operators, such as + (addition) or * (multiplication). For example, if you wanted to multiply two cells, such as C3 and D3, and then divide the product by 3, you would design a formula that looks like this:

```
=(C3*D3)/3
```

Notice that the formula begins with the equal sign (=). This lets Excel know that the information that you are placing in the cell is meant to do a calculation. The parentheses are used to let Excel know that you want C3 multiplied by D3 before the result is divided by 3. Creating appropriate formulas requires an understanding of the order of mathematical operations, or what is often called the rules of precedence. The natural order of math operations is covered in the next section.

As previously mentioned, you can create formulas that add, subtract, and multiply cells in the worksheet. Table 4.1 lists some of the operators that you can use and how you would use them in a simple formula.

**Table 4.1**    Excel's Mathematical Operators

| Operator | Performs | Sample Formula | Result |
|----------|----------|----------------|--------|
| ^ | Exponentiation | =A1^3 | Enters the result of raising the value in cell A1 to the third power |
| + | Addition | =A1+A2 | Enters the total of the values in cells A1 and A2 |
| − | Subtraction | =A1–A2 | Subtracts the value in cell A2 from the value in cell A1 |
| * | Multiplication | =A2*A3 | Multiplies the value in cell A2 by cell A3 |
| / | Division | =A1/B1 | Divides the value in cell A1 by the value in cell B1 |

Figure 4.1 shows some formulas that have been created for an Excel worksheet. So that you can see how I wrote the formulas, I've configured Excel so that it shows the formula that has been placed in a cell

rather than the results of the formula (which is what you would normally see).

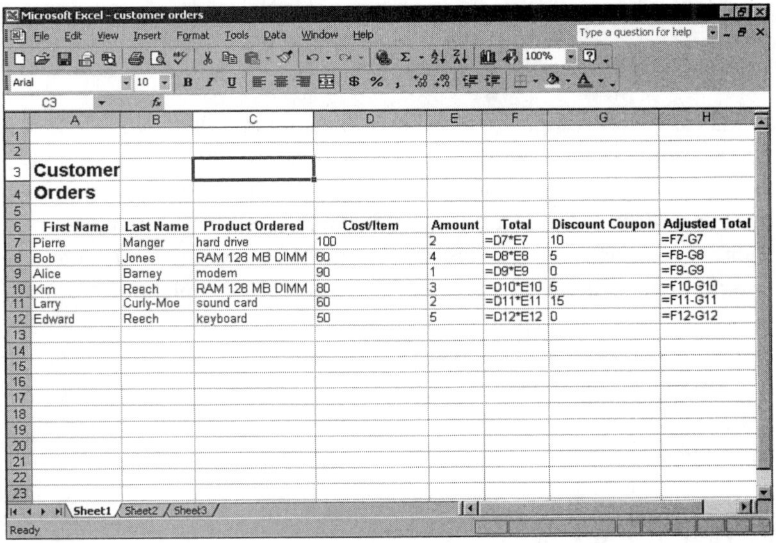


| | A | B | C | D | E | F | G | H |
|---|---|---|---|---|---|---|---|---|
| 1 | | | | | | | | |
| 2 | | | | | | | | |
| 3 | Customer | | | | | | | |
| 4 | Orders | | | | | | | |
| 5 | | | | | | | | |
| 6 | First Name | Last Name | Product Ordered | Cost/Item | Amount | Total | Discount Coupon | Adjusted Total |
| 7 | Pierre | Manger | hard drive | 100 | 2 | =D7*E7 | 10 | =F7-G7 |
| 8 | Bob | Jones | RAM 128 MB DIMM | 80 | 4 | =D8*E8 | 5 | =F8-G8 |
| 9 | Alice | Barney | modem | 90 | 1 | =D9*E9 | 0 | =F9-G9 |
| 10 | Kim | Reech | RAM 128 MB DIMM | 80 | 3 | =D10*E10 | 5 | =F10-G10 |
| 11 | Larry | Curly-Moe | sound card | 60 | 2 | =D11*E11 | 15 | =F11-G11 |
| 12 | Edward | Reech | keyboard | 50 | 5 | =D12*E12 | 0 | =F12-G12 |

**FIGURE 4.1**

*You can create formulas to do simple calculations in your worksheets.*

## ORDER OF OPERATIONS

The order of operations, or *operator precedence*, simply means that some operations take precedence over other operations in a formula. For example, in the formula =C2+D2*E2, the multiplication of D2 times E2 takes precedence, so D2 is multiplied by E2 and then the value in cell C2 is added to the result.

You can force the precedence of an operation by using parentheses. For example, if you want C2 and D2 added before they are multiplied by E2, the formula would have to be written =(C2+D2)*E2.

The natural order of math operators follows:

| | |
|---|---|
| 1st | Exponent (^) and calculations within parentheses |
| 2nd | Multiplication (*)and division (/) |
| 3rd | Addition (+) and subtraction (−) |

In the case of operations such as multiplication and division, which operate at the same level in the natural order, a formula containing the multiplication operator followed by the division operator will execute these operators in the order they appear in the formula from left to right. If you don't take this order into consideration, you could run into problems when entering your formulas. For example, if you want to determine the average of the values in cells A1, B1, and C1, and you enter =A1+B1+C1/3, you'll get the wrong answer. The value in C1 will be divided by 3, and that result will be added to A1+B1. To determine the total of A1 through C1 first, you must enclose that group of values in parentheses: =(A1+B1+C1)/3.

## ENTERING FORMULAS

You can enter formulas in one of two ways: by typing the entire formula, including the cell addresses, or by typing the formula operators and selecting the cell references. Take a look at both ways.

To type a formula, perform the following steps:

1. Select the cell where you will place the formula.

2. Type an equal sign (=) into the cell to begin the formula.

3. Enter the appropriate cell references and operators for the formula. Figure 4.2 shows a simple multiplication formula. The formula also appears in the Formula bar as you type it. The cells that you specify in the formula are highlighted with a colored border.

4. Press **Enter** when you have finished the formula, and Excel calculates the result.

**TIP**

**Unwanted Formula**     If you start to enter a formula and then decide you don't want to use it, you can skip entering the formula by pressing **Esc**.

| SUM | ▾ X ✓ *f*ₓ | =D7*E7 | | | | | | | |
|---|---|---|---|---|---|---|---|---|---|
| | A | B | C | D | E | F | G | H | I |
| 1 | | | | | | | | | |
| 2 | | | | | | | | | |
| 3 | **Customer** | | | | | | | | |
| 4 | **Orders** | | | | | | | | |
| 5 | | | | | | | | | |
| 6 | **First Name** | **Last Name** | **Product Ordered** | **Cost/Item** | **Amount** | **Total** | **Discount Coupon** | **Adjusted Total** | |
| 7 | Pierre | Manger | hard drive | 100 | 2 | =D7*E7 | 10 | | |
| 8 | Bob | Jones | RAM 128 MB DIMM | 80 | 4 | | 5 | | |
| 9 | Alice | Barney | modem | 90 | 1 | | 0 | | |
| 10 | Kim | Reech | RAM 128 MB DIMM | 80 | 3 | | 5 | | |
| 11 | Larry | Curly-Moe | sound card | 60 | 2 | | 15 | | |
| 12 | Edward | Reech | keyboard | 50 | 5 | | 0 | | |
| 13 | | | | | | | | | |
| 14 | | | | | | | | | |
| 15 | | | | | | | | | |

**FIGURE 4.2**
*The formula appears in the cell and in the Formula bar as you type it.*

To enter a formula by selecting cell addresses, follow these steps:

1. Click in the cell where you will place the formula.

2. Type the equal sign (=) to begin the formula.

3. Click the cell whose address you want to appear first in the formula. You also can click a cell in a different worksheet or workbook. The cell address appears in the cell and in the Formula bar.

4. Type a mathematical operator after the value to indicate the next operation you want to perform. The operator appears in the cell and in the Formula bar.

5. Continue clicking cells and typing operators until the formula is complete.

6. Press **Enter** to accept the formula and have Excel place its results into the cell.

**CAUTION**

> **Error!**   If ERR appears in a cell, you've likely made a mistake somewhere in the formula. Be sure you did not commit one of these common errors: dividing by zero, using a blank cell as a divisor, referring to a blank cell, deleting a cell used in a formula, or including a reference to the same cell in which the formula appears.

**TIP**

> **Natural Language Formulas**   Excel also enables you to create what are called Natural Language formulas. You can refer to a cell by its column heading name and the corresponding row label. For example, if you had a column labeled Total and a column labeled Discount for each customer, you can write a formula such as =Smith Total–Smith Discount. You are referring to cells by the labels that you have placed in the worksheet rather than the actual cell addresses.

## USING THE STATUS BAR AUTOCALCULATE FEATURE

Using a feature that Excel calls AutoCalculate, you can view the sum of a column of cells simply by selecting the cells and looking at the status bar. The values in the selected cells are added. You also can right-click the AutoCalculate area of the status bar and choose different formulas, such as average, minimum, maximum, and count.

This feature is useful if you want to quickly check the total for a group of cells or compute the average. It also allows you to "try out" an Excel function (discussed in Lesson 5) before actually entering it into a cell. You also can view the average, minimum, maximum, and count of a range of cells. To display something other than the sum, highlight the group of cells on which you want the operation performed, right-click the status bar, and select the option you want from the shortcut menu that appears (see Figure 4.3).

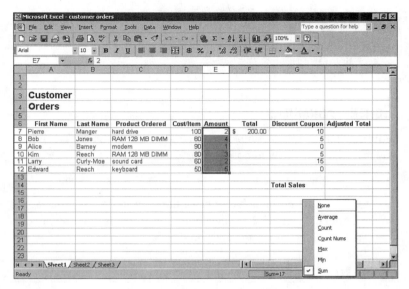

**FIGURE 4.3**
*You can view the results of different built-in formulas in the status bar.*

TIP

> **Where's the Status Bar?**    If the status bar is not visible on your screen, you can display it by selecting the **View** menu and then selecting **Status Bar**.

## DISPLAYING FORMULAS

Normally, Excel does not display the formula in a cell. Instead, it displays the result of the calculation. You can view the formula by selecting the cell and looking in the Formula bar. However, if you're trying to review all the formulas in a large worksheet, it would be easier if you could see them all at once (and even print them). If you want to view formulas in a worksheet, follow these steps:

1. Open the **Tools** menu and choose **Options**.

2. Click the **View** tab.

3. In the Window options area of the View tab (near the bottom of the tab), click to select the **Formulas** check box.

4. Click **OK**.

## EDITING FORMULAS

Editing a formula is the same as editing any entry in Excel. The following steps show how to do it:

1. Select the cell that contains the formula you want to edit.

2. Click in the Formula bar to place the insertion point in the formula, or press **F2** to enter Edit mode (the insertion point is placed at the end of the entry in that cell).

**TIP**

**In-Cell Editing**   To quickly edit the contents of a cell, double-click the cell. The insertion point appears inside the cell, and you can make any necessary changes.

3. Press the left-arrow key or the right-arrow key to move the insertion point within the formula. Then, use the **Backspace** key to delete characters to the left, or use the **Delete** key to delete characters to the right. Type any additional characters.

4. When you finish editing the data, click the **Enter** button on the Formula bar or press **Enter** to accept your changes.

In this lesson, you learned how to enter and edit formulas. In the next lesson, you learn how to copy formulas, when to use relative and absolute cell addresses, and how to change Excel's settings for calculating formulas in the worksheet.

# Lesson 5

# Manipulating Formulas and Understanding Cell References

*In this lesson, you learn how to copy formulas, use relative and absolute cell references, and change calculation settings.*

## Copying Formulas

Copying labels and values in Excel is no big deal. You can use the Copy and Paste commands (discussed in Lesson 10, "Editing Worksheets") or you can use some of the Fill features discussed in Lesson 3, "Entering Data into the Worksheet." Copying or moving formulas, however, is a little trickier.

Suppose that you create the formula =D7*E7 and place it into cell F7, as shown in Figure 5.1. You have designed the formula to reference cells D7 and E7. However, Excel looks at these cell references a little differently. Excel sees cell D7 as the entry that is located two cells to the left of F7 (where the formula has been placed, in this example). It sees cell E7 as being the location that is one cell to the left of F7.

Excel's method of referencing cells is called *relative referencing.* The great thing about this method of referencing cells is that, when you copy a formula to a new location, it adjusts to the relative cell references around it and provides you with the correct calculation.

For example, you could copy the formula in cell F7 to cell F8, and Excel would use relative referencing to change the cell addresses in

the formula. The original formula =D7*E7 would appear as D8*D7
when copied to cell F8.

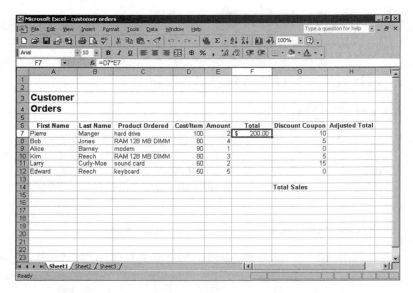

**FIGURE 5.1**
*Formulas you place in Excel use relative referencing for calculations.*

Relative referencing is very useful in most situations where you copy
a formula to several cells in the same column. However, it can get you
into trouble when you cut and paste a formula to a new location or
copy the formula to a location where it can no longer reference the
appropriate cells to provide you with the correct calculation. In these
situations, you must use absolute referencing so that the formula references only specified cells and does not change the cell references in
the formula when pasted to the new location. Absolute referencing is
discussed in the next section.

You can copy formulas using the Copy and Paste commands (see
Lesson 10); however, when you need to copy a formula to multiple
locations, you also can use the Fill feature discussed in Lesson 3.

Because Excel uses relative referencing by default, the formula adjusts to each of its new locations. An alternative way to "copy" a formula to multiple adjacent cells is to select all cells that will contain the formula before you actually write the formula in the first cell. Follow these steps:

1. Select all the cells that will contain the formula (dragging so that the cell that you will write the formula in is the first of the selected group of cells).

2. Enter the formula into the first cell.

3. Press **Ctrl+Enter** and the formula is placed in all the selected cells.

### GET AN ERROR?

If you get an error message in a cell after copying a formula, verify the cell references in the copied formula. For more information on sorting out cell referencing, see the next section in this lesson.

## USING RELATIVE AND ABSOLUTE CELL ADDRESSES

As mentioned at the beginning of this lesson, when you copy a formula from one place in the worksheet to another, Excel adjusts the cell references in the formulas relative to their new positions in the worksheet. There might be occasions when you don't want Excel to change the reference related to a particular cell that appears in a formula (or in an Excel function, which is discussed in Lesson 6, "Performing Calculations with Functions").

### ABSOLUTE VERSUS RELATIVE

An *absolute reference* is a cell reference in a formula that does not change when copied to a new location. A *relative reference* is a cell reference in a formula that is adjusted when the formula is copied.

For example, suppose you have a worksheet that computes the commission made on sales by each of your salespeople. Sales have been so good that you've decided to give each person on the sales team a $200 bonus. Figure 5.2 shows the worksheet that you've created.

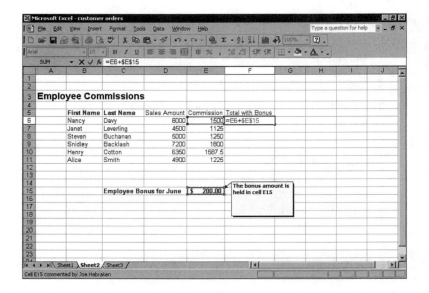

**FIGURE 5.2**
*Some formulas require absolute references.*

Notice that the bonus amount is contained in only one cell on the worksheet (cell E15). Therefore, when you create the formula that will be used in F6 and then copied to cells F7 through F11, you need to be sure that the bonus amount in cell E15 is always referenced by the formula. This is a case where you must "absolutely" reference the bonus amount in cell E15.

To make a cell reference in a formula absolute, add a $ (dollar sign) before the column letter and before the row number that make up the cell address. For example, in Figure 4.2, the formula in F6 must read as follows:

`=E6+$E$15`

The address, $E$15, refers to cell E15, meaning that cell E15 is absolutely referenced by the formula. This cell reference remains "locked" even when you copy the formula to the other cells in the E column.

To create an absolute reference in a formula (or a function, which is discussed in Lesson 6), create your formula as you normally would (as detailed in Lesson 4, "Performing Simple Calculations"). After typing or pointing out a cell address in a formula that needs to be an absolute reference, press **F4**. A dollar sign ($)is placed before the cell and row designation for that cell.

Some formulas might contain cell addresses where you will make the column designation absolute, but not the row (or vice versa). For example, you could have a formula $A2/2. You are telling Excel that the values always will be contained in column A (it is absolute), but the row reference (2) can change when the formula is copied. Having a cell address in a formula that contains an absolute designation and a relative reference is called a *mixed reference*.

**PLAIN ENGLISH**

**Mixed References**   A reference that is only partially absolute, such as A$2 or $A2. When a formula that uses a mixed reference is copied to another cell, only part of the cell reference (the relative part) is adjusted.

Absolute referencing and mixed references are required by some of Excel's built-in functions as well. You work with functions in the next lesson.

## RECALCULATING THE WORKSHEET

Excel automatically recalculates the results in your worksheet every time you enter a new value or edit a value or formula. This is fine for most workbooks. However, if you have a computer with limited memory and processing power, you might find that having Excel recalculate all the results in a very large worksheet every time you make a change means that you are sitting and waiting for Excel to complete the recalculation.

You can turn off the automatic recalculation. However, this won't be necessary except in situations where you are working with huge workbooks that contain a large number of formulas, functions, and data. Turning off the automatic calculation feature also means that you must remember to manually recalculate the values in the worksheet before you print. To change the recalculation setting, take the following steps:

1. Open the **Tools** menu and choose **Options**.

2. Click the **Calculation** tab to display the options shown in Figure 5.3.

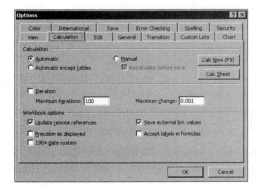

**FIGURE 5.3**
*You can turn off the automatic recalculation feature.*

**3.** Select one of the following Calculation options:

- **Automatic**—This is the default setting. It recalculates the entire workbook each time you edit or enter a formula.

- **Automatic Except Tables**—This automatically recalculates everything except formulas in a data table.

- **Manual**—This option tells Excel to recalculate only when you say so. To recalculate manually, press the **F9** key. When this option is selected, you can turn off or on the Recalculate Before Save option.

**4.** Click **OK**.

In this lesson, you learned how to copy formulas. You also learned when to use relative and absolute cell addresses and how to change the recalculation settings. In the next lesson, you learn how to use the Insert Function feature to insert Excel's special built-in formulas called functions.

# LESSON 6

# Performing Calculations with Functions

*In this lesson, you learn how to perform calculations with functions and how to use the Insert Function feature to quickly insert functions into your worksheets.*

## WHAT ARE FUNCTIONS?

You already learned in Lesson 4, "Performing Simple Calculations," how to create your own formulas in Excel. When you work with more complex calculations, you are better off using Excel's built-in formulas—functions.

Functions are ready-made formulas that perform a series of operations on a specified range of values. For example, to determine the sum of a series of numbers in cells A1 through H1, you can enter the function =SUM(A1:H1). Excel functions can do all kinds of calculations for all kinds of purposes, including financial and statistical calculations.

Every function consists of the following three elements:

- The = sign, which indicates that what follows is a function (formula).

- The function name, such as SUM, which indicates the operation to be performed.

- A list of cell addresses, such as (A1:H1), which are to be acted upon by the function. Some functions can include more than one set of cell addresses, which are separated by commas (such as A1,B1,H1).

You can enter functions into the worksheet by typing the function and cell references (as you did with your own formulas), or you can use the Insert Function feature, which walks you through the process of creating a function in a worksheet (you will work with the Insert Function feature in a moment). Table 6.1 lists some of the Excel functions that you probably will use most often in your worksheets.

**Table 6.1** Commonly Used Excel Functions

| Function | Example | Description |
|---|---|---|
| AVERAGE | =AVERAGE(B4:B9) | Calculates the mean or average of a group of cell values. |
| COUNT | =COUNT(A3:A7) | Counts the number of cells that hold values in the selected range or group of cells. This also can be used to tell you how many cells are in a particular column, which tells you how many rows are in your spreadsheet. |
| IF | =IF(A3>=1000,"BONUS", "NO BONUS") | Allows you to place a conditional function in a cell. In this example, if A3 is greater than or equal to 1000, the true value, BONUS, is used. If A3 is less than 1000, the false value, NO BONUS, is placed in the cell. |

**Table 6.1**  (continued)

| Function | Example | Description |
|----------|---------|-------------|
| MAX | =MAX(B4:B10) | Returns the maximum value in a range of cells. |
| MIN | =MIN(B4:B10) | Returns the minimum value in a range of cells. |
| PMT | =PMT(.0825/12,360, 180000) | Calculates the monthly payment on a 30-year loan (360 monthly payments) at 8.25% a year (.0825/12 a month) for $180,000. |
| SUM | =SUM(A1:A10) | Calculates the total in a range of cells. |

**TIP**

> **Specify Text with Quotation Marks**    When entering text into a function, the text must be enclosed within quotation marks. For example, in the function =IF(A5>2000 "BONUS","NO BONUS"), if the condition is met (the cell value is greater than 2000), the word BONUS will be returned by the function. If the condition is not met, the phrase NO BONUS will be returned in the cell by the function.

Excel provides a large number of functions listed by category. There are Financial functions, Date and Time functions, Statistical functions, and Logical functions (such as the IF function described in Table 6.1). The group of functions that you use most often depends on the type of worksheets you typically build. For example, if you do a lot of accounting work, you will find that the Financial functions offer functions for computing monthly payments, figuring out the growth on an investment, and even computing the depreciation on capital equipment.

Although some commonly used functions have been defined in Table 6.1, as you become more adept at using Excel, you might want to explore some of the other functions available. Select **Help**, **Microsoft Excel Help**. On the Contents tab of the Help window, open the **Function Reference** topic. Several subtopics related to Excel functions and their use are provided.

## USING AUTOSUM

Adding a group of cells probably is one of the most often-used calculations in an Excel worksheet. Because of this fact, Excel makes it very easy for you to place the SUM function into a cell. Excel provides the AutoSum button on the Standard toolbar. AutoSum looks at a column or row of cell values and tries to select the cells that should be included in the SUM function.

To use AutoSum, follow these steps:

1. Select the cell where you want to place the SUM function. Typically, you will choose a cell that is at the bottom of a column of values or at the end of a row of data. This makes it easy for AutoSum to figure out the range of cells that it should include in the SUM function.

2. Click the **AutoSum** button on the Standard toolbar. AutoSum inserts =SUM and the cell addresses that it thinks should be included in the function (see Figure 6.1).

$$\boxed{\Sigma}$$

3. If the range of cell addresses that AutoSum selected is incorrect, use the mouse to drag and select the appropriate group of cells.

4. Press the **Enter** key. AutoSum calculates the total for the selected range of cells.

| SUM | ▼ X ✔ ƒ | =SUM(H7:H13) | | | | | |
|---|---|---|---|---|---|---|---|

|  | A | B | C | D | E | F | G | H |
|---|---|---|---|---|---|---|---|---|
| 1 |  |  |  |  |  |  |  |  |
| 2 |  |  |  |  |  |  |  |  |
| 3 | **Customer** |  |  |  |  |  |  |  |
| 4 | **Orders** |  |  |  |  |  |  |  |
| 5 |  |  |  |  |  |  |  |  |
| 6 | First Name | Last Name | Product Ordered | Cost/Item | Amount | Total | Discount Coupon | Adjusted Total |
| 7 | Pierre | Manger | hard drive | 100 | 2 | $ 200.00 | 10 | $ 190.00 |
| 8 | Bob | Jones | RAM 128 MB DIMM | 80 | 4 | $ 320.00 | 5 | $ 315.00 |
| 9 | Alice | Barney | modem | 90 | 1 | $ 90.00 | 0 | $ 90.00 |
| 10 | Kim | Reech | RAM 128 MB DIMM | 80 | 3 | $ 240.00 | 5 | $ 235.00 |
| 11 | Larry | Curly-Moe | sound card | 60 | 2 | $ 120.00 | 15 | $ 105.00 |
| 12 | Edward | Reech | keyboard | 50 | 5 | $ 250.00 | 0 | $ 250.00 |
| 13 |  |  |  |  |  |  |  |  |
| 14 |  |  |  |  |  |  | Total Sales | =SUM(H7:H13) |
| 15 |  |  |  |  |  |  |  |  |
| 16 |  |  |  |  |  |  |  |  |
| 17 |  |  |  |  |  |  |  |  |
| 18 |  |  |  |  |  |  |  |  |
| 19 |  |  |  |  |  |  |  |  |
| 20 |  |  |  |  |  |  |  |  |
| 21 |  |  |  |  |  |  |  |  |
| 22 |  |  |  |  |  |  |  |  |
| 23 |  |  |  |  |  |  |  |  |

H ◄ ► H \ Sheet1 / Sheet2 / Sheet3 /

Edit

**FIGURE 6.1**

*AutoSum inserts the SUM function and selects the cells that will be totaled by the function.*

**TIP**

**Quick AutoSum**    To bypass the step where Excel displays the SUM formula and its arguments in the cell, select the cell in which you want the sum inserted and double-click the **AutoSum** button on the Standard toolbar.

## USING THE INSERT FUNCTION FEATURE

After you become familiar with a function or a group of functions, you place a particular function in an Excel worksheet by typing the function name and the cells to be referenced by the function (the same as you have done for formulas that you create as outlined in Lesson 4). However, when you are first starting out with functions, you will find it much easier to create them using the Insert Function feature. The Insert Function feature leads you through the process of inserting

a function and specifying the appropriate cell addresses in the
function.

For example, suppose you want to compute the average, maximum,
and minimum of a group of cells that contain the weekly commissions
for your sales force. Figure 6.2 shows how these three functions
would look on a worksheet (the display has been changed in Excel to
show you the functions rather than their results). You could use the
Insert Function feature to create any or all of these functions.

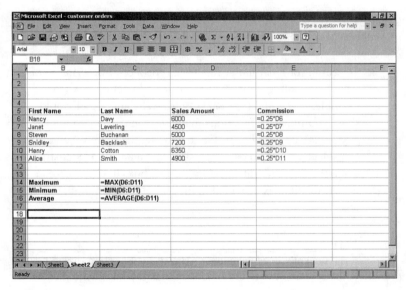

**FIGURE 6.2**
*Functions can be placed into a worksheet using the Insert Function feature.*

To use the Insert Function feature, follow these steps:

1. Click in the cell where you want to place the function.

2. Click the **Insert Function** button on the Formula bar. The
   Insert Function dialog box appears (see Figure 6.3).

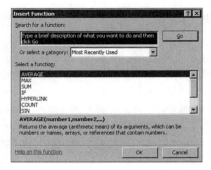

**FIGURE 6.3**
*The Insert Function dialog box helps you select the function you want to use.*

**3.** To search for a particular function, type a brief description of what you want to do in the Search for a Function box (for example, you could type `monthly payment` and Excel would show you financial functions that help you calculate monthly payments), and then click **Go** to conduct the search. You also can select a function category, such as Financial or Statistical, using the Select a Category drop-down box. In either case, a list of functions is provided in the Select a Function dialog box.

**TIP**

> **Recently Used Functions**    The Insert Function dialog box by default lists the functions that you have used most recently.

**4.** From the Functions list, select the function you want to insert. Then click **OK**. The Function Arguments dialog box appears. This dialog box allows you to specify the range of cells (some functions require multiple ranges of cells) that the function acts upon (see Figure 6.4).

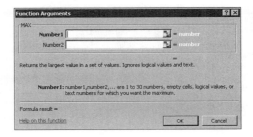

**FIGURE 6.4**
*The Function Arguments dialog box is where you specify the cells that will be
acted upon by the function. The argument specified in this case is for the
Maximum function.*

5. Next, you must enter the range of cells that will be acted
   upon by the function. Click the **Collapse** button on the far
   right of the Number1 text box in the Function Arguments dialog box. This returns you to the worksheet.

6. Use the mouse to select the cells that you want to place in the
   function (see Figure 6.5). Then click the **Expand** button on
   the right of the Function Arguments dialog box.

7. Click **OK**. Excel inserts the function and cell addresses for
   the function into the selected cell and displays the result.

If you find that you would like to edit the list of cells acted upon by a
particular function, select the cell that holds the function and click the
**Insert Function** button on the Formula bar. The Function Arguments
dialog box for the function appears. Select a new range of cells for the
function, as discussed in steps 4 and 5.

**NOTE**

> **What's This Function?**  If you'd like to know more about
> a particular function, click the **Help on This Function** link
> at the bottom of the Function Arguments dialog box.
> The Help window will open with help on this specific
> function.

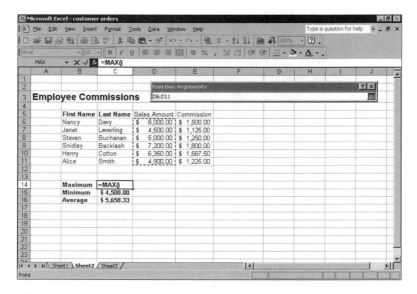

**FIGURE 6.5**
*The Function Arguments collapses and allows you to select the cells that will be acted upon by the function.*

In this lesson, you learned the basics of working with functions, and you learned how to use Excel's Insert Function feature to quickly enter functions. You also learned how to quickly total a series of numbers with the AutoSum tool. In the next lesson, you learn how to move around in an Excel worksheet.

# LESSON 7
# Getting Around in Excel

*In this lesson, you learn the basics of moving around in a worksheet and within a workbook.*

## MOVING FROM WORKSHEET TO WORKSHEET

Now that you've taken a look at how to enter labels, values, formulas, and functions, you should take a look at how to navigate the space provided by Excel workbooks and worksheets. By default, each workbook starts off with three worksheets. You can add or delete worksheets from the workbook as needed. Because each workbook consists of one or more worksheets, you need a way of moving easily from worksheet to worksheet. Use one of the following methods:

- Click the tab of the worksheet you want to go to (see Figure 7.1). If the tab is not shown, use the tab scroll buttons to bring the tab into view, and then click the tab.

- Press **Ctrl+PgDn** to move to the next worksheet or **Ctrl+PgUp** to move to the previous one.

## SWITCHING BETWEEN WORKBOOKS

Switching between the different workbooks that you have open on the Windows desktop is very straightforward. By default, each workbook has its own button on the Windows taskbar and opens in its own Excel application window (refer to Figure 7.1). To switch between workbooks, click the button for the workbook you want.

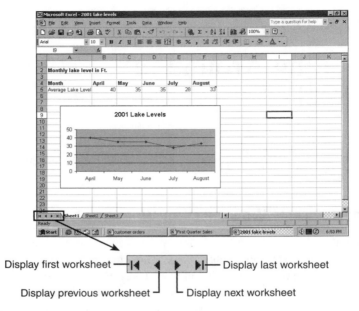

Display first worksheet ——— Display last worksheet
Display previous worksheet —— —— Display next worksheet

**FIGURE 7.1**
*Use the tabs to move from worksheet to worksheet.*

If you don't want to have a separate taskbar entry for each open Excel workbook, you can turn off this feature using the Windows in Taskbar option on the View tab of the Options dialog box (click **Tools**, **Options**). Keep in mind, however, that disabling this feature means that you will have to use the Window menu to switch between Excel workbooks. To do so, select the Window menu, and then select the name of the workbook you want to make the current workbook in the Excel application window.

## MOVING WITHIN A WORKSHEET

To enter your worksheet data, you need some way of moving to the various cells within the worksheet. Keep in mind that the part of the worksheet displayed onscreen is only a small piece of the actual worksheet.

## USING THE KEYBOARD

To move around the worksheet with your keyboard, use the key combinations listed in Table 7.1.

**Table 7.1**  Moving Around a Worksheet with the Keyboard

| To Move | Press This |
| --- | --- |
| Up one cell | Up-arrow key |
| Down one cell | Down-arrow key |
| Right one cell | Right-arrow key |
| Left one cell | Left-arrow key |
| Up one screen | Page Up |
| Down one screen | Page Down |
| Leftmost cell in a row (column A) | Home |
| Lower-right corner of the data area | Ctrl+End |
| Cell A1 | Ctrl+Home |
| Last occupied cell to the right of a row | End+right-arrow key |

You also can quickly go to a specific cell address in a worksheet using the Go To feature. Press **Ctrl+G** (or select **Edit, Go To**). Type the cell address you want to go to into the Reference box, and then click the **OK** button (see Figure 7.2).

**FIGURE 7.2**
*The Go To feature can be used to move to a specific cell address on the worksheet.*

The Go To feature keeps a list of cells to which you have recently moved using the Go To feature. To quickly move to a particular cell in the Go To list, double-click that cell address.

TIP

**Even Faster Than Go To**    To move quickly to a specific cell on a worksheet, type the cell's address (the column letter and row number; for example, **C25**) into the Name box at the left end of the Formula bar and press **Enter**.

## USING A MOUSE

To scroll through a worksheet with a mouse, follow the techniques listed in Table 7.2.

**Table 7.2**    Moving Around a Worksheet with the Mouse

| To Move | Click This |
| --- | --- |
| Move the selector to a particular cell. | Any cell. |
| View one more row, up or down. | Up or down arrows on the vertical scrollbar. |
| View one more column, left or right. | Left or right arrows on the horizontal scrollbar. |
| Move through a worksheet quickly. | The vertical or horizontal scrollbar; drag it up or down or right and left, respectively. As you drag, a ScreenTip displays the current row/column number. |

TIP

**Watch the Scroll Box**    The size of the scroll box changes to represent the amount of the total worksheet that is currently visible. If the scroll box is large, you know you're seeing almost all of the current worksheet in the window. If the scroll box is small, most of the worksheet is currently hidden from view.

## USING A WHEEL-ENABLED MOUSE

If you use the Microsoft IntelliMouse or any wheel-enabled mouse, you can move through a worksheet even faster than you can using the scrollbars and a conventional mouse. Here's how:

| To: | Do This: |
| --- | --- |
| Scroll a few rows (scroll up and down) | Rotate the wheel in the middle of the mouse forward or backward. |
| Scroll faster (pan) | Click and hold the wheel button, and then drag the mouse in the direction in which you want to pan. The farther away from the origin mark (the four-headed arrow) you drag the mouse, the faster the panning action. To slow the pan, drag the mouse back toward the origin mark. |
| Pan without holding the wheel | Click the wheel once, and then move the mouse in the direction in which you want to pan. (You'll continue to pan when you move the mouse until you turn panning off by clicking the wheel again.) |
| Zoom in and out | Press the **Ctrl** key as you rotate the middle wheel. If you zoom out, you can click any cell you want to jump to. You then can zoom back in so you can see your data. |

In this lesson, you learned how to move through a worksheet, and to move from workbook to workbook. In the next lesson, you learn how to get help in Excel.

# LESSON 8
# Getting Help in Microsoft Excel

*In this lesson, you learn how to access and use the Help system in Microsoft Excel.*

## HELP: WHAT'S AVAILABLE?

Microsoft Excel supplies a Help system that makes it easy for you to look up information on Excel commands and features as you create your worksheets and work with the various Excel features. Because every person is different, the Help system can be accessed in several ways. You can

- Ask a question in the Ask a Question box.

- Ask the Office Assistant for help.

- Get help on a particular element you see onscreen with the What's This? tool.

- Use the Contents, Answer Wizard, and Index tabs in the Help window to get help.

- Access the Office on the Web feature to view Web pages containing help information (if you are connected to the Internet).

## USING THE ASK A QUESTION BOX

The Ask a Question box is a new way to quickly open the Excel Help system. The Ask a Question box resides at the top right of the Excel application window.

For example, if you are working in Excel and wish to view information on how to create a new chart, type **How do I create a chart?** into the Ask a Question box. Then press the **Enter** key. A shortcut menu appears below the Ask a Question box, as shown in Figure 8.1.

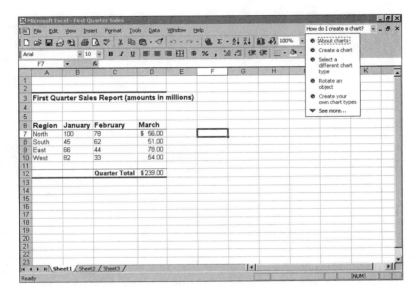

**FIGURE 8.1**
*The Ask a Question box provides a list of Help topics that you can access quickly.*

To access one of the Help topics supplied on the shortcut menu, click that particular topic. The Help window opens with topical matches for that keyword or phrase displayed.

In the case of the "new chart" question used in Figure 8.1, you could select **Create a chart** from the shortcut menu that appears. This opens the help window and displays help on how to create an Excel chart (see Figure 8.2).

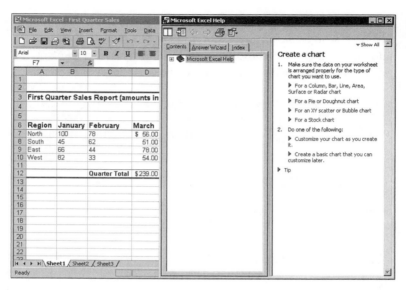

**FIGURE 8.2**
*The Ask a Question box provides a quick way to access the Help window.*

In the Help window, you can use the links provided to navigate the Help system. Click any of the content links to expand the information provided on that particular topic. You also can use the Contents, Answer Wizard, and Index tabs to find additional information or look for new information in the Help window. You learn more about these different Help window tabs later in this lesson.

## USING THE OFFICE ASSISTANT

Another way to get help in Excel is to use the Office Assistant. The Office Assistant supplies the same type of access to the Help system as the Ask a Question box. You ask the Office Assistant a question, and it supplies you with a list of possible answers that provide links to various Help topics. The next two sections discuss how to use the Office Assistant.

## TURNING THE OFFICE ASSISTANT ON AND OFF

By default, the Office Assistant is off. To show the Office Assistant in your application window, select the **Help** menu, and then select **Show the Office Assistant**.

You also can quickly hide the Office Assistant if you no longer want it in your application window. Right-click the Office Assistant and select **Hide**. If you want to get rid of the Office Assistant completely so it isn't activated when you select the Help feature, right-click the Office Assistant and select **Options**. Clear the **Use the Office Assistant** check box, and then click **OK**. You can always get the Office Assistant back by selecting **Help**, **Show Office Assistant**.

## ASKING THE OFFICE ASSISTANT A QUESTION

When you click the Office Assistant, a balloon appears above it. Type a question into the text box. For example, you might type **How do I print?** for help printing your work. Click the **Search** button.

The Office Assistant provides some topics that reference Help topics in the Help system. Click the option that best describes what you're trying to do. The Help window appears, containing more detailed information. Use the Help window to get the exact information you need.

Although not everyone likes the Office Assistant because having it enabled means that it is always sitting in your Excel application window, it can be useful at times. For example, when you access particular features in Excel, the Office Assistant can automatically provide you with context-sensitive help on that particular feature. If you are brand new to Microsoft Excel, you might want to use the Office Assistant to help you learn the various features that Excel provides as you use them.

**TIP**

**Select Your Own Office Assistant**    Several different Office Assistants are available in Microsoft Excel. To select your favorite, click the Office Assistant and select the **Options** button. On the Office Assistant dialog box that appears, select the **Gallery** tab. Click the **Next** button repeatedly to see the different Office Assistants available. When you locate the assistant you want to use, click **OK**.

## USING THE HELP WINDOW

You also can forego either the Type a Question box or the Office Assistant and get your help directly from the Help window. To directly access the Help window, select **Help** and then **Microsoft Excel Help**. You also can press the **F1** key to make the Help window appear.

The Help window provides two panes. The pane on the left provides three tabs: Contents, Answer Wizard, and Index. The right pane of the Help window provides either help subject matter or links to different Help topics. It functions a great deal like a Web browser window. You click a link to a particular body of information and that information appears in the right pane.

The first thing you should do is maximize the Help window by clicking its **Maximize** button. This makes it easier to locate and read the information the Help system provides (see Figure 8.3).

When you first open the Help window, a group of links in the right pane provides you with access to information about new Excel features and other links, such as a link to Microsoft's Office Web site. Next, take a look at how you can take advantage of different ways to find information in the Help window: the Contents tab, the Answer Wizard tab, and the Index tab.

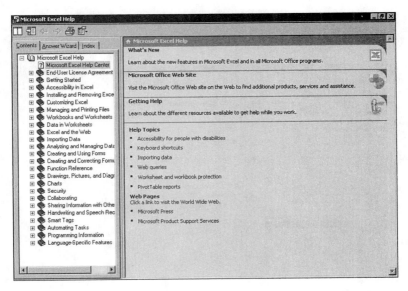

**FIGURE 8.3**
*The Help window provides access to all the help information provided for Excel.*

**TIP**

> **View the Help Window Tabs**   If you don't see the differ-
> ent tabs in the Help window, click the **Show** button on
> the Help window toolbar.

## USING THE CONTENTS TAB

The Contents tab of the Help system is a series of books you can
open. Each book has one or more Help topics in it, which appear as
pages or chapters. To select a Help topic from the Contents tab, follow
these steps:

1. In the Help window, click the **Contents** tab on the left side of
   the Help window.

2. Find the book that describes, in broad terms, the subject for
   which you need help.

**3.** Double-click the book, and a list of Help topics appears below the book, as shown in Figure 8.4.

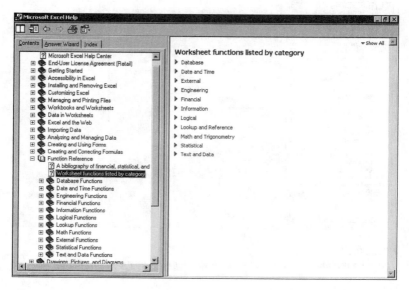

**FIGURE 8.4**
*Use the Contents tab to browse through the various Help topics.*

**4.** Click one of the pages (the pages contain a question mark) under a Help topic to display it in the right pane of the Help window. Expand any of the links provided to read more information as needed.

**5.** When you finish reading a topic, select another topic on the Contents tab or click the Help window's **Close** (**x**) button to exit Help.

## USING THE ANSWER WIZARD

Another way to get help in the Help window is to use the Answer Wizard. The Answer Wizard works the same as the Ask a Question box or the Office Assistant; you ask the wizard a question and it supplies you with a list of topics that relate to your question. You click one of the choices provided to view help in the Help window.

To get help using the Answer Wizard, follow these steps:

1. Click the **Answer Wizard** tab in the Help window.

2. Type your question into the What Would You Like to Do? box. For example, you might type the question, **How do I copy a formula?**

3. After typing your question, click the **Search** button. A list of topics appears in the Select Topic to Display box. Select a particular topic, and its information appears in the right pane of the Help window, as shown in Figure 8.5.

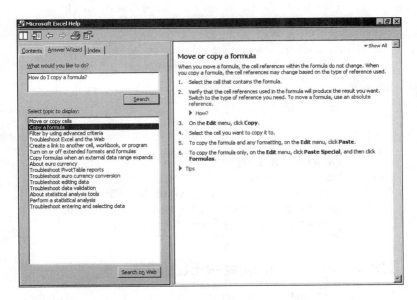

**FIGURE 8.5**
*Search for help in the Help window using the Answer Wizard tab.*

**TIP**

> **Print Help**    If you want to print information provided in the Help window, click the **Print** icon on the Help toolbar.

## USING THE INDEX

The Index is an alphabetical listing of every Help topic available. It's like an index in a book.

Follow these steps to use the index:

1. In the Help window, click the **Index** tab.

2. Type the first few letters of the topic for which you are looking. The Or Choose Keywords box jumps quickly to a keyword that contains the characters you have typed.

3. Double-click the appropriate keyword in the keywords box. Topics for that keyword appear in the Choose a Topic box.

4. Click a topic to view help in the right pane of the Help window (see Figure 8.6).

**TIP**

> **Navigation Help Topics**    You can move from topic to topic in the right pane of the Help window by clicking the various links that are provided there. Some topics are collapsed. Click the triangle next to the topic to expand the topic and view the help provided.

## GETTING HELP WITH SCREEN ELEMENTS

If you wonder about the function of a particular button or tool on the Excel screen, wonder no more. Just follow these steps to learn about this part of Help:

1. Select **Help** and then **What's This?** or press **Shift+F1**. The mouse pointer changes to an arrow with a question mark.

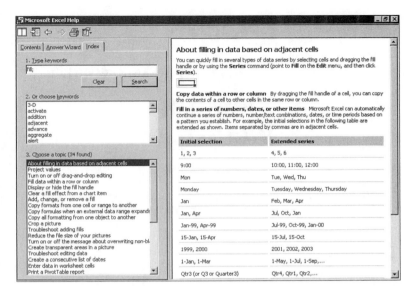

**FIGURE 8.6**
*Use the Index tab to get help in the Help window.*

2. Click the screen element for which you want help. A box appears explaining the element.

**TIP**

> **Take Advantage of ScreenTips**    Another Help feature provided by Excel is the ScreenTip. All the buttons on the different toolbars provided by Excel have a ScreenTip. Place the mouse on a particular button or icon, and the name of the item (which often helps you determine its function) appears in a ScreenTip.

In this lesson, you learned how to use the Excel Help feature. In the next lesson, you learn how to use different views of your Excel worksheets.

## LESSON 9
# Different Ways to View Your Worksheet

*In this lesson, you learn about the various ways in which you can view your worksheets.*

## CHANGING THE WORKSHEET VIEW

There are many ways to change how your worksheet appears within the Excel window. Changing the view has no effect on how your worksheets look when printed (unless you choose to hide data onscreen). However, changing the view and getting a different perspective helps you to see the overall layout of the worksheet and allows you to view worksheet cells that might not appear in the default screen view. For example, you can enlarge or reduce the size of the worksheet so that you can view more or less of it at one time.

`100%` ▾ To enlarge or reduce your view of the current worksheet, use the Zoom feature. Simply click the **Zoom** button on the Standard toolbar and select the zoom percentage you want to use from the following: 25%, 50%, 75%, 100%, or 200%. If you want to zoom by a number that's not listed, just type the number into the Zoom box and press **Enter**.

You also can have Excel zoom in on a particular portion of a worksheet. This is particularly useful when you have created very large worksheets. Select the area of the worksheet you want to zoom in on, and then click the **Zoom** button list and click **Selection**. You then can select different zoom values on the Zoom list to zoom in or out on that particular portion of the worksheet. Keep in mind that Excel zooms in on the entire worksheet, not just the selected cells. (It just makes sure that you can see the selected cells when you change the zoom values.)

**TIP**

**Fast Zoom with a Wheel Mouse** If you use the Microsoft IntelliMouse or another compatible wheel mouse, you can zoom in and out quickly by holding down the **Ctrl** key as you move the wheel forward or back.

You also can display your worksheet so that it takes up the full screen. This eliminates all the other items in the Excel window, such as the toolbars, the Formula bar, the status bar, and so on. Figure 9.1 shows a worksheet in the Full Screen view. To use this view, select the **View** menu and select **Full Screen**. To return to Normal view, click **Close Full Screen**.

| | File | Edit | View | Insert | Format | Tools | Data | Window | Help | | | | _ B X |
|---|---|---|---|---|---|---|---|---|---|---|---|---|
| | A | B | C | D | E | F | G | H | | | | |
| 1 | | | | | | | | | | | | |
| 2 | | | | | | | | | | | | |
| 3 | **Customer** | | | | | | | | | | | |
| 4 | **Orders** | | | | | | | | | | | |
| 5 | | | | | | | | | | | | |
| 6 | **First Name** | **Last Name** | **Product Ordered** | **Cost/Item** | **Amount** | **Total** | **Discount Coupon** | **Adjusted Total** | | | | |
| 7 | Pierre | Manger | hard drive | 100 | 2 | $ 200.00 | 10 | $ 190.00 | | | | |
| 8 | Bob | Jones | RAM 128 MB DIMM | 80 | 4 | $ 320.00 | 5 | $ 315.00 | | | | |
| 9 | Alice | Barney | modem | 90 | 1 | $ 90.00 | 0 | $ 90.00 | | | | |
| 10 | Kim | Reech | RAM 128 MB DIMM | 80 | 3 | $ 240.00 | 5 | $ 235.00 | | | | |
| 11 | Larry | Curly-Moe | sound card | 60 | 2 | $ 120.00 | 15 | $ 105.00 | | | | |
| 12 | Edward | Reech | keyboard | 50 | 5 | $ 250.00 | 0 | $ 250.00 | | | | |
| 13 | | | | | | | | | | | | |
| 14 | | | | | | | Total Sales | $ 1,185.00 | | | | |
| 15 | | | | | | | | | | | | |
| 16 | | | | | | | | | | | | |
| 17 | | Full Scree ▼ X | | | | | | | | | | |
| 18 | | Close Full Screen | | | | | | | | | | |
| 19 | | | | | | | | | | | | |
| 20 | | | | | | | | | | | | |
| 21 | | | | | | | | | | | | |
| 22 | | | | | | | | | | | | |
| 23 | | | | | | | | | | | | |
| 24 | | | | | | | | | | | | |
| 25 | | | | | | | | | | | | |
| 26 | | | | | | | | | | | | |
| 27 | | | | | | | | | | | | |
| 28 | | | | | | | | | | | | |
| 29 | | | | | | | | | | | | |
| 30 | | | | | | | | | | | | |

**FIGURE 9.1**

*View your worksheet on the entire screen.*

## FREEZING COLUMN AND ROW LABELS

When you work with very large worksheets, it can be very annoying as you scroll to the right or down through the worksheet when you can no longer see your row headings or column headings, respectively. For example, you might be entering customer data where the customer's name is in the first column of the worksheet, and when you scroll to the extreme right to enter data, you can no longer see the customer names.

You can freeze your column and row labels so that you can view them no matter how far you scroll down or to the right in your worksheet. For example, Figure 9.2 shows frozen row headings that allow you to see the customer names no matter how far you move to the right of the worksheet.

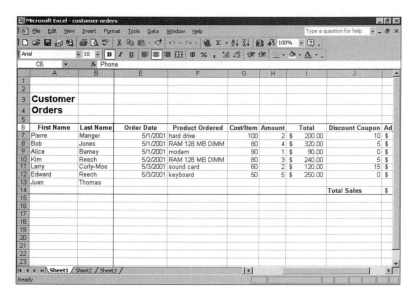

**FIGURE 9.2**
*You can freeze row and column headings so they remain onscreen as you scroll.*

To freeze row or column headings (or both), follow these steps:

1. Click the cell to the right of the row labels and/or below any column labels you want to freeze. This highlights the cell.

2. Select the **Window** menu, and then select **Freeze Panes**.

You might want to experiment on a large worksheet. Freeze the column and row headings, and then use the keyboard or the mouse to move around in the worksheet. As you do, the row and/or column headings remain locked in their positions. This enables you to view data in other parts of the worksheet without losing track of what that data represents.

When you have finished working with the frozen column and row headings, you easily can unfreeze them. Select the **Window** menu again and select **Unfreeze Panes**.

## SPLITTING WORKSHEETS

When you work with very large worksheets, you might actually want to split the worksheet into multiple windows. This enables you to view the same worksheet in different windows. You then can scroll through the multiple copies of the same worksheet and compare data in cells that are normally far apart in the worksheet.

Figure 9.3 shows a worksheet that has been split into multiple panes. Each "copy" of the worksheet will have its own set of vertical and horizontal scrollbars.

To split a worksheet, follow these steps:

1. Click in the cell where you want to create the split. A split appears to the left of the selected cell and above the selected cell.

2. You can adjust the vertical or horizontal split bars using the mouse. Place the mouse on the split bar and drag it to a new location.

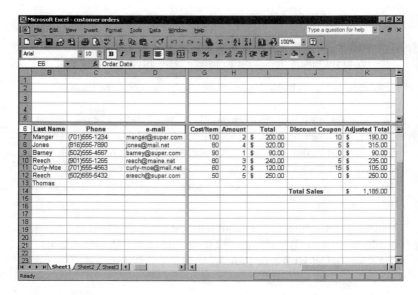

**FIGURE 9.3**
*You can split a worksheet into two windows, making it easy to compare data in the worksheet.*

3. You can use the scrollbars in the different split panes to view data in the worksheet (different data can be viewed in each pane).

To remove the split, select the **Window** menu and select **Remove Split**.

**TIP**

> **Create Splits with the Split Boxes**   You also can create a vertical or horizontal split in a worksheet by using the split boxes. A horizontal split box rests just above the vertical scrollbar, and a vertical split box rests on the far right of the horizontal scrollbar. Place your mouse on either of these split boxes and drag them onto the work-sheet to create a split bar.

# Hiding Workbooks, Worksheets, Columns, and Rows

For those times when you're working on top-secret information (or at least information that is somewhat proprietary, such as employee salaries), you can hide workbooks, worksheets, columns, or rows from prying eyes. For example, if you have confidential data stored in one particular worksheet, you can hide that worksheet, yet still be able to view the other worksheets in that workbook. You also can hide particular columns or rows within a worksheet.

Use these methods to hide data:

- To hide a row or a column in a worksheet, click a row or column heading to select it (you can select adjacent columns or rows by dragging across them). Then, right-click within the row or column and select **Hide** from the shortcut menu that appears (see Figure 9.4). To unhide the row or column, right-click the border between the hidden item and rows or columns that are visible, and then select **Unhide** from the shortcut menu.

- To hide a worksheet, click its tab to select it. Then, open the **Format** menu and select **Sheet**, **Hide**. To unhide the worksheet, select **Format**, **Sheet**, and then **Unhide**. Select the worksheet to unhide in the Unhide dialog box that appears, and then click **OK**.

- To hide an entire workbook, open the **Window** menu and select **Hide**. This removes the workbook from the Excel window, even though the workbook is open. To unhide the workbook, select **Window**, **Unhide**.

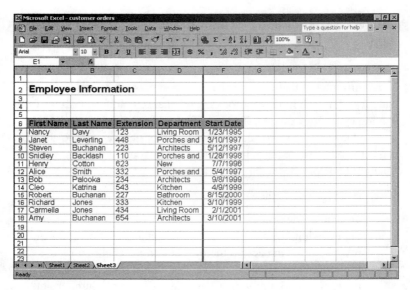

**FIGURE 9.4**
*Column E, which contains employee salaries, has been hidden on a worksheet.*

## LOCKING CELLS IN A WORKSHEET

In some situations, you might create a worksheet or worksheets and someone else will enter the data. In these situations, you might want to lock cells that contain formulas and functions so that the person doing the data entry does not accidentally overwrite or delete the worksheet formulas or functions. Locking cells in a worksheet is a two-step process. You must first select and lock the cells. Then, you must turn on protection on the entire worksheet for the "lock" to go into effect.

Follow these steps to lock cells on a worksheet:

1. Select the cells in the worksheet that you want to lock. These are typically the cells that contain formulas or functions.

2. Select **Format** and then **Cells**. The Format Cells dialog box appears. Click the **Protection** tab on the dialog box (see Figure 9.5).

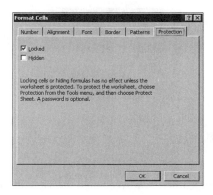

**FIGURE 9.5**
*Cells can be locked using the Protection tab of the Format Cells dialog box.*

3. Be sure the Locked check box is selected on the Protection tab. Then click **OK**.

4. Now you must protect the entire worksheet to have the lock feature protect the cells that you selected. Select the **Tools** menu, point at **Protections**, and then select **Protect Sheet**. The Protect Sheet dialog box appears (see Figure 9.6).

5. Enter a password if you want to require a password for "unprotecting" the worksheet. Then click **OK**.

The cells that you locked in steps 1, 2, and 3 no longer will accept data entry. Every time someone tries to enter data into one of those cells, Excel displays a message stating that data will not be accepted. The cells now are protected and you can pass the workbook on to the person who handles the data entry.

**FIGURE 9.6**
*The worksheet must be protected if you want to lock cells containing formulas or functions.*

In this lesson, you learned how to change the view of your worksheet, freeze column and row headings, and hide data. You also learned how to lock certain cells from data entry. In the next lesson, you will learn how to edit worksheets by correcting data. You also will learn to use the spell checker and AutoCorrect feature.

# LESSON 10
# Editing Worksheets

*In this lesson, you learn how to change data and how to undo those changes if necessary. You also learn how to search for data and replace it with other data, how to spell check your work, and how to copy, move, and delete data.*

## CORRECTING DATA

You've taken a look at entering text, values, formulas, and functions. There will definitely be occasions when you need to edit information in a cell. One way to change an entry in a cell is to replace it by selecting the cell and then entering new data. Just press **Enter** after entering the information. If you just want to modify the existing cell content, you also can edit data within a cell.

To edit information in a cell, follow these steps:

1.  Select the cell in which you want to edit data.

2.  To begin editing, click in the Formula bar to place the insertion point into the cell entry. To edit within the cell itself, press **F2** or double-click the cell. This puts you in Edit mode; the word Edit appears in the status bar.

3.  Press the right- or left-arrow key to move the insertion point within the entry. Press the **Backspace** key to delete characters to the left of the insertion point; press the **Delete** key to delete characters to the right. Then, type any characters you want to add.

4.  Press the **Enter** key when you have finished making your changes.

If you change your mind and you no longer want to edit your entry, click the **Cancel** button on the Formula bar or press **Esc**.

**TIP**

**Moving to the Beginning or End of a Cell Entry**    In Edit mode, you can move quickly to the beginning or end of a cell's contents. Press **Home** to move to the beginning of the entry; press **End** to move to the end of the entry.

## UNDOING AN ACTION

Although editing a worksheet is supposed to improve it, you might find that you've done something to a cell or range of cells that you had not intended. This is where the Undo feature comes in.

 You can undo just about any action while working in Excel, including any changes you make to a cell's data. To undo a change, click the **Undo** button on the Standard toolbar (or select **Edit**, **Undo**).

 You also can undo an undo. Just click the **Redo** button on the Standard toolbar.

**TIP**

**Undoing/Redoing More Than One Thing**    The Undo button undoes only the most recent action. To undo several previous actions, click the **Undo** button multiple times or click the drop-down arrow on the undo button and select the number of actions you want undone.

## USING THE REPLACE FEATURE

Suppose you've entered a particular label or value into the worksheet and find that you have consistently entered it incorrectly. A great way to change multiple occurrences of a label or value is using Excel's

Replace feature; you can locate data in the worksheet and replace it with new data. To find and replace data, follow these steps:

1. Select the **Edit** menu, and then select **Replace**. The Find and Replace dialog box appears, as shown in Figure 10.1.

**FIGURE 10.1**
*Find and replace data with the Find and Replace dialog box.*

2. Type the text or value that you want to find into the **Find What** text box.

3. Click in the **Replace With** text box and type the text you want to use as replacement text.

4. To expand the options available to you in the dialog box, click the **Options** button (Figure 10.1 shows the dialog box in its expanded form).

5. If you want to match the exact case of your entry so that Excel factors in capitalization, click the **Match Case** check box. If you want to locate cells that contain exactly what you entered into the Find What text box (and no additional data), click the **Match Entire Cell Contents** check box.

6. To search for entries with particular formatting, click the **Format** button to the right of the Find What box. The Find Format dialog box appears (see Figure 10.2). You can search for entries that have been assigned number, alignment, font, border, patterns, and protection using the appropriate tab on

the Find Format dialog box. After making your selection, click the **OK** button.

**FIGURE 10.2**
*The Find Format dialog box enables you to search for entries that have been assigned a particular formatting.*

7. You also can replace your entries with a particular formatting. Click the **Format** button to the right of the Replace With box. The Replace Format dialog box appears. It is the same as the Find Format dialog box. Simply select any formats you want to assign to your replacement, and then click **OK**.

8. Click **Find Next** to find the first occurrence of your specified entry.

9. When an occurrence is found, it is highlighted. Click **Replace** to replace only this occurrence and then click **Find Next** to find the next occurrence.

10. If you want to find all the occurrences, click **Find All**; you also can replace all the occurrences of the entry with **Replace All**.

11. When you have finished working with the Find and Replace dialog box, click **Close**.

**NOTE**

> **Search an Entire Workbook**    If you want to search an entire workbook for a particular entry, click the **Within** drop-down list in the Find and Replace dialog box and select **Workbook**.

If you don't need to replace an entry but would like to find it in the worksheet, you can use the Find feature. Select **Edit**, **Find**, and then type the data you want to locate into the Find What text box and click **Find Next**.

## CHECKING YOUR SPELLING

Because worksheets also include text entries, you might want to make sure that you check for any misspellings in a worksheet before printing the data. Excel offers a spell-checking feature that finds and corrects misspellings in a worksheet.

To run the Spelling Checker, follow these steps:

1. Click the **Spelling** button on the Standard toolbar (or select **Tools**, **Spelling**). The Spelling dialog box appears. Excel finds the first misspelled word and displays it at the top of the Spelling dialog box. A suggested correction appears in the Suggestions box (see Figure 10.3).

2. To accept the suggestion in the Suggestions box, click **Change**, or click **Change All** to change all occurrences of the misspelled word.

3. If the suggestion in the Suggestions box is not correct, you can do any of the following:

   • Select a different suggestion from the Suggestions box, and then click **Change** or **Change All**.

   • Type your own correction into the Change To box, and then click **Change** or **Change All**.

- Click **Ignore Once** to leave the word unchanged.

- Click **Ignore All** to leave all occurrences of the word unchanged.

- Click **Add to Dictionary** to add the word to the dictionary so that Excel won't flag it as misspelled again.

- Click **AutoCorrect** to add a correctly spelled word to the AutoCorrect list so that Excel can correct it automatically as you type.

- If you make a mistake related to a particular entry, click the **Undo Last** button to undo the last change you made.

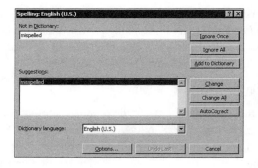

**FIGURE 10.3**
*Correct spelling mistakes with the options in the Spelling dialog box.*

4. You might see a message asking whether you want to continue checking spelling at the beginning of the sheet. If so, click **Yes** to continue. When the Spelling Checker can't find any more misspelled words, it displays a prompt telling you that the spelling check is complete. Click **OK** to confirm that the spelling check is finished.

**NOTE**

**Setting Spelling Options**    If you want to set options related to the Spelling feature, such as ignoring words in uppercase and words with numbers, click the **Options** button in the Spelling dialog box. This takes you to the Options dialog box for the Speller. Set options as needed and then click **OK** to return to the Spelling dialog box.

## COPYING AND MOVING DATA

In Lesson 3, you learned how to use the Fill feature to copy a particular entry to multiple cells. In this section, you take a closer look at the Copy feature. When you copy or cut data in a cell, that data is held in a temporary storage area (a part of the computer's memory) called the Clipboard.

Excel 2002 makes it easy for you to work with the Clipboard because it can be viewed in the Office Clipboard task pane (you look at the Clipboard later in this lesson). This enables you to keep track of items that you have copied or cut to the Clipboard. The Clipboard not only enables you to copy or move data with Excel, but it enables you to place Excel data directly into another application such as Word.

**PLAIN ENGLISH**

**Clipboard**    The Clipboard is an area of memory that is accessible to all Windows programs. The Clipboard is used to copy or move data from place to place within a program or between programs.

When you copy data, you create a duplicate of data in a cell or range of cells. Follow these steps to copy data:

1.  Select the cell(s) that you want to copy. You can select any range or several ranges if you want. (See Lesson 13, "Working with Ranges," for more information).

2. Click the **Copy** button on the Standard toolbar. The contents of the selected cell(s) are copied to the Clipboard.

3. Select the first cell in the area where you would like to place the copy. (To copy the data to another worksheet or workbook, change to that worksheet or workbook first.)

4. Click the **Paste** button. Excel inserts the contents of the Clipboard at the location of the insertion point.

CAUTION

**Watch Out!**   When copying or moving data, be careful not to paste the data over existing data (unless, of course, you intend to).

You can copy the same data to several places by repeating the **Paste** command. Items remain on the Clipboard until you remove them.

## USING DRAG AND DROP

The fastest way to copy something is to drag and drop it. Select the cells you want to copy, hold down the **Ctrl** key, and drag the border of the range you selected (see Figure 10.4). When you release the mouse button, the contents are copied to the new location. To insert the data between existing cells, press **Ctrl+Shift** as you drag.

To drag a copy to a different sheet, press **Ctrl+Alt** as you drag the selection to the sheet's tab. Excel switches you to that sheet, where you can drop your selection into the appropriate location.

## MOVING DATA

Moving data is similar to copying except that the data is removed from its original place and placed into the new location.

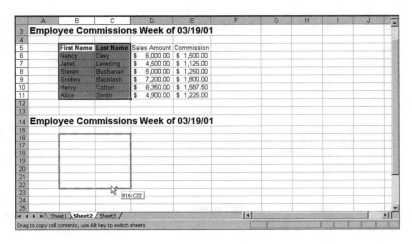

**FIGURE 10.4**
*Dragging is the fastest way to copy data.*

To move data, follow these steps:

1. Select the cells you want to move.

2. Click the **Cut** button.

3. Select the first cell in the area where you want to place the data. To move the data to another worksheet, change to that worksheet.

4. Click **Paste**.

## USING DRAG AND DROP TO MOVE DATA

You also can move data using drag and drop. Select the data to be moved, and then drag the border of the selected cells to its new location. To insert the data between existing cells, press **Shift** while you drag. To move the data to a different worksheet, press the **Alt** key and drag the selection to the worksheet's tab. You're switched to that sheet, where you can drop your selection at the appropriate point.

# USING THE OFFICE CLIPBOARD

You can use the Office Clipboard to store multiple items that you cut or copy from an Excel worksheet (or workbook). You then can paste or move these items within Excel or to other Office applications. The Office Clipboard can hold up to 24 items.

**CAUTION**

**What a Drag!**   You can't use the Drag-and-Drop feature to copy or move data to the Office Clipboard.

The Office Clipboard is viewed in the Clipboard task Pane. Follow these steps to open the Office Clipboard:

1.  Select the **Edit** menu, and then select **Office Clipboard**. The Clipboard task pane appears. Any items that you have cut or copied appear on the Clipboard (see Figure 10.5).

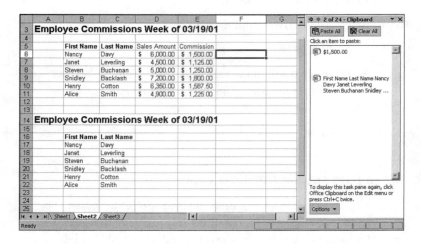

**FIGURE 10.5**
*The Clipboard provides a list of items that you have cut or copied.*

2. To paste an item that appears on the Clipboard, click in a cell on the worksheet, and then click the item on the Clipboard. It then is pasted into the selected cell.

You can remove any of the items from the Clipboard. Place the mouse pointer on an item listed on the Clipboard and click the drop-down arrow that appears. Click **Delete** on the shortcut menu that appears.

You also can clear all the items from the Clipboard. Click the **Clear All** button at the top of the Clipboard task pane.

**TIP**

> **Open the Clipboard from the System Tray**   You can quickly open the Office Clipboard in any Office application by double-clicking the Clipboard icon in the Windows System Tray (at the far right of the Windows taskbar).

## DELETING DATA

To delete the data in a cell or range of cells, select them and press **Delete**. Excel also offers some additional options for deleting cells and their contents:

- With the **Edit, Clear** command, you can delete only the formatting of a cell (or an attached comment) without deleting its contents. The formatting of a cell includes the cell's color, border style, numeric format, font size, and so on. You'll learn more about this option in a moment.

- With the **Edit, Delete** command, you can remove cells and then shift surrounding cells over to take their place (this option is described in more detail in Lesson 14, "Inserting and Removing Cells, Rows, and Columns").

To use the Clear command to remove the formatting of a cell or a note, follow these steps:

1. Select the cells you want to clear.

2. Open the **Edit** menu and point at **Clear**. The Clear submenu appears.

3. Select the desired Clear option: **All** (which clears the cells of all contents, formatting, and notes), **Formats**, **Contents**, or **Comments**.

In this lesson, you learned how to edit cell data and undo changes. In addition, you learned how to spell check your worksheet and how to copy, move, and delete data. In the next lesson, you learn how to format your Excel labels and values.

# LESSON 11
# Changing How Numbers and Text Look

*In this lesson, you learn how to customize the appearance of numbers in your worksheet and how to customize your text formatting to achieve the look you want.*

## FORMATTING TEXT AND NUMBERS

When you work in Excel, you work with two types of formatting: value formatting and font formatting. Value formatting is where you assign a particular number style to a cell (or cells) that holds numeric data. You can assign a currency style, a percent style, and several other numeric styles to values.

Another formatting option available to you in Excel relates to different font attributes. For example, you can add bold or italic to the contents of a cell or cells. You also can change the font used for a range of cells or increase the font size.

Next, you take a look at numeric formatting, and then you look at how different font attributes are controlled in Excel.

## USING THE STYLE BUTTONS TO FORMAT NUMBERS

The Formatting toolbar (just below the Standard toolbar) contains several buttons for applying a format to your numbers, including the following:

| Button | Name | Example/Description |
|--------|------|---------------------|
| $ | Currency Style | $1,200.90 |
| % | Percent Style | 20.90% |
| , | Comma Style | 1,200.90 |
| +.0 .00 | Increase Decimal | Adds one decimal place |
| .00 +.0 | Decrease Decimal | Deletes one decimal place |

To use one of these buttons, select the cell or cells you want to format, and then click the desired button. If you would like more formatting options for numeric values, read on; they are covered in the next section.

## NUMERIC FORMATTING OPTIONS

The numeric values that you place in your Excel cells are more than just numbers; they often represent dollar amounts, a date, or a percentage. If the various numeric style buttons on the Formatting toolbar (discussed in the previous section) do not offer the exact format you want for your numbers, don't worry. Excel's Format Cells dialog box offers a wide range of number formats and even allows you to create custom formats.

To use the Format Cells dialog box to assign numeric formatting to cells in a worksheet, follow these steps:

1. Select the cell or range that contains the values you want to format.

2. Select the **Format** menu and select **Cells**. The Format Cells dialog box appears.

3. Click the **Number** tab. The different categories of numeric formats are displayed in a Category list (see Figure 11.1).

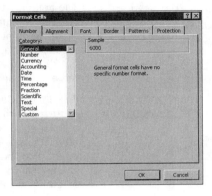

**FIGURE 11.1**
*Apply a numeric format in the Number tab of the Format Cells dialog box.*

4. In the Category list, select the numeric format category you want to use. The sample box displays the default format for that category.

5. Click **OK** to assign the numeric format to the selected cells.

As you can see from the Number tab on the Format Cells dialog box, Excel offers several numeric formatting styles. Table 11.1 provides a list of these different number formats.

**Table 11.1**    Excel's Number Formats

| Number Format | Examples | Description |
|---|---|---|
| General | 10.6 $456,908.00 | Excel displays your value as you enter it. In other words, this format displays currency or percent signs only if you enter them yourself. |

**Table 11.1**    (continued)

| Number Format | Examples | Description |
|---|---|---|
| Number | 3400.50<br>_120.39 | The default Number format has two decimal places. Negative numbers are preceded by a minus sign, but they also can appear in red and/or parentheses. |
| Currency | $3,400.50<br>_$3,400.50 | The default Currency format has two decimal places and a dollar sign. Negative numbers appear with a minus sign, but they also can appear in red and/or parentheses. |
| Accounting | $3,400.00<br>$978.21 | Use this format to align dollar signs and decimal points in a column. The default Accounting format has two decimal places and a dollar sign. |
| Date | 11/7 | The default Date format is the month and day separated by a slash; however, you can select from numerous other formats. |
| Time | 10:00 | The default Time format is the hour and minutes separated by a colon; however, you can opt to display seconds, a.m., or p.m. |
| Percentage | 99.50% | The default Percentage format has two decimal places. Excel multiplies the value in a cell by 100 and displays the result with a percent sign. |

**Table 11.1**   (continued)

| Number Format | Examples | Description |
|---|---|---|
| Fraction | 1/2 | The default Fraction format is up to one digit on each side of the slash. Use this format to display the number of digits you want on each side of the slash and the fraction type (such as halves, quarters, eighths, and so on). |
| Scientific | 3.40E+03 | The default Scientific format has two decimal places. Use this format to display numbers in scientific notation. |
| Text | 135RV90 | Use Text format to display both text and numbers in a cell as text. Excel displays the entry exactly as you type it. |
| Special | 02110 | This format is specifically designed to display ZIP codes, phone numbers, and Social Security numbers correctly so that you don't have to enter any special characters, such as hyphens. |
| Custom | 00.0% | Use Custom format to create your own number format. You can use any of the format codes in the Type list and then make changes to those codes. The # symbol represents a number placeholder, and 0 represents a zero placeholder. |

You also can open the Format Cell dialog box using a shortcut menu. Select the cell or cells that you want to assign a numeric format to, and then right-click those cells. On the shortcut menu that appears, select **Format Cells**. Then, select the **Number** tab to select your numeric format.

**CAUTION**

> **That's Not the Date I Entered!**   If you enter a date into a cell that is already formatted with the Number format, the date appears as a value that represents the number of days between January 1, 1900 and that date. Change the cell's formatting from a Number format to a Date format and select a date type. The entry in the cell then appears as an actual date.

**TIP**

> **How Do I Get Rid of a Numeric Format?**   To remove a number format from a cell (and return it to General format), select the cell whose formatting you want to remove, open the **Edit** menu, select **Clear**, and select **Formats**.

## HOW YOU CAN MAKE TEXT LOOK DIFFERENT

When you type text into a cell, Excel automatically formats it in the Arial font with a text size of 10 points. The 12-point font size is considered typical for business documents (the higher the point size, the bigger the text is; there are approximately 72 points in an inch). You can select from several fonts (such as Baskerville, Modern, or Rockwell) and change the size of any font characters in a cell. You can also apply special font attributes, such as bold, italic, and underline.

**PLAIN ENGLISH**

**Font**    A font is a set of characters that have the same typeface, which means they are of a single design (such as Times New Roman).

Before you take a look at applying different font attributes to the cells in a worksheet, take a look at how you change the default font for all your Excel workbooks. This enables you to select a different font and font size for your worksheets.

To change the default font, follow these steps:

1. Select **Tools** and then click **Options** to open the Options dialog box.

2. Click the **General** tab (see Figure 11.2).

3. In the Standard Font area, use the drop-down list to select a new font. Use the Size drop-down list to select a new default font size.

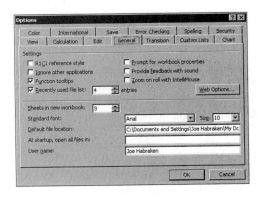

**FIGURE 11.2**
*You can set a new default font and font size for your Excel workbooks.*

4. When you click the **OK** button, Excel makes your preference the default font and size.

## CHANGING TEXT ATTRIBUTES WITH TOOLBAR BUTTONS

When you are working on your various Excel worksheets, you probably will apply a variety of formatting options to the different cells in a particular worksheet. A fast way to assign text attributes, such as bold and italic, is to use the various font attribute buttons on the Excel Formatting toolbar.

To use the Formatting toolbar to change text attributes, follow these steps:

1.  Select the cell or range that contains the text whose look you want to change.

2.  To change the font, click the **Font** drop-down list, and select a new font name. To change the font size, click the **Font Size** drop-down list and select the size you want to use. You also can type the point size into the Font Size box and then press **Enter**.

3.  To add an attribute such as bold, italic, or underlining to the selected cells, click the appropriate button: **Bold**, **Italic**, or **Underline**, respectively.

 **TIP**

> **Font Keyboard Shortcuts**    You can apply certain attributes quickly by using keyboard shortcuts. First select the cell(s), and then press **Ctrl+B** for bold, **Ctrl+I** for italic, **Ctrl+U** for single underline, or **Ctrl+5** for strikethrough.

You also can change the color of the font in a cell or cells. Select the cell or cells and click the **Font Color** drop-down arrow on the Formatting toolbar. Select a font color from the Color palette that appears.

## ACCESSING DIFFERENT FONT ATTRIBUTES

If you would like to access a greater number of font format options for a cell or range of cells, you can use the Font tab of the Format Cells dialog box. It provides access to different fonts, font styles, font sizes, font colors, and other text attributes, such as strikethrough and super-script/subscript. To format cells using the Font tab of the Format Cells dialog box, follow these steps:

1. Select the cell or range that contains the text you want to format.

2. Select the **Format** menu and select **Cells**, or press **Ctrl+1**. (You can also right-click the selected cells and choose **Format Cells** from the shortcut menu.)

3. Click the **Font** tab. The Font tab provides drop-down lists and check boxes for selecting the various font attributes (see Figure 11.3).

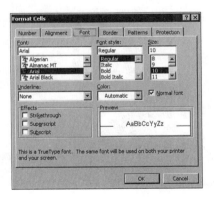

**FIGURE 11.3**
*The Font tab provides access to all the font attributes.*

4. Select the options you want.

5. Click **OK** to close the dialog box and return to your worksheet.

## ALIGNING TEXT IN CELLS

When you enter data into a cell, that data is aligned automatically. Text is aligned on the left, and numbers are aligned on the right (values resulting from a formula or function are also right-aligned). Both text and numbers are initially set at the bottom of the cells. However, you can change both the vertical and the horizontal alignment of data in your cells.

Follow these steps to change the alignment:

1. Select the cell or range you want to align.

2. Select the **Format** menu and then select **Cells**. The Format Cells dialog box appears.

3. Click the **Alignment** tab (see Figure 11.4).

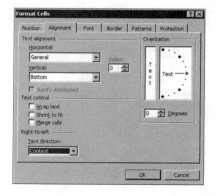

**FIGURE 11.4**
*Select from the Alignment options on the Alignment tab of the Format Cells dialog box.*

4. Choose from the following options to set the alignment:

   • **Horizontal**—Lets you specify a left/right alignment in the cells. (The **Center Across** selection centers a title or other text within a range of cells, which is discussed in a moment.)

- **Vertical**—Lets you specify how you want the text aligned in relation to the top and bottom of the cells.

- **Orientation**—Lets you flip the text sideways or print it from top to bottom instead of left to right.

- **Wrap Text**—Tells Excel to wrap long lines of text within a cell without changing the width of the cell. (Normally, Excel displays all text in a cell on one line.)

- **Shrink to Fit**—Shrinks the text to fit within the cell's current width. If the cell's width is adjusted, the text increases or decreases in size accordingly.

- **Merge Cells**—Combines several cells into a single cell. All data is overlaid, except for the cell in the upper-left corner of the selected cells.

5. Click **OK** when you have finished making your selections.

**TIP**

**Changing Text Orientation**    The Alignment tab also provides an Orientation box that enables you to rotate text within a cell or a group of merged cells. Drag the degree dial on the Alignment tab or use the Degree box to specify the amount of rotation for the text.

## ALIGNING TEXT FROM THE TOOLBAR

Like the font attributes such as bold and italic, you also can select certain alignment options directly from the Formatting toolbar. The following buttons enable you to align the text:

| Button | Name | Description |
| --- | --- | --- |
| ≡ | Align Left | Places data at left edge of cell |
| ≡ | Align Right | Places data at right edge of cell |

| Button | Name | Description |
|---|---|---|
| ≡ | Center | Centers data in cell |
| ⊞ | Merge and Center | Centers data in selected cell range |

Excel also enables you to indent your text within a cell. If you're typing a paragraph's worth of information into a single cell, for example, you can indent that paragraph by selecting **Left Alignment** from the Horizontal list box in the Format Cells dialog box (as explained earlier). After selecting Left Alignment, set the amount of indent you want with the Indent spin box in the Format Cells dialog box.

In addition, you can add an indent quickly by clicking the following buttons on the Formatting toolbar:

| Button | Name | Description |
|---|---|---|
| ⇥ | Decrease Indent | Removes an indent or creates a negative indent |
| ⇤ | Increase Indent | Adds an indent |

## COMBINING CELLS AND WRAPPING TEXT

You can also center text across a range of cells or merge several cells to hold a sheet title or other text information. If you want to center a title or other text over a range of cells, select the entire range of blank cells in which you want the text centered. This should include the cell that contains the text you want to center (which should be in the cell on the far left of the cell range). Then, click the **Merge and Center** button on the Formatting toolbar.

Combining a group of cells also allows you to place a special heading or other text into the cells (this works well in cases where you use a large font size for the text). Select the cells that you want to combine. Then, select **Format**, **Cells** and select the **Alignment** tab of the Format Cells dialog box.

Click the **Merge Cells** check box and then click **OK**. The cells are then merged.

If you have a cell or a group of merged cells that holds a large amount of text (such as an explanation), you might want to wrap the text within the cell or merged cells. Click the cell that holds the text entry, and then select **Format**, **Cells**. Select the **Alignment** tab of the Format Cells dialog box.

Click the **Wrap Text** checkbox. Then click **OK**.

## COPYING FORMATS WITH FORMAT PAINTER

After applying a numeric format or various font attributes to a cell or cell range, you can easily copy those formatting options to other cells. This works whether you're copying numeric or text formatting or shading or borders, as you'll learn in upcoming lessons. To copy a format from one cell to another, follow these steps:

1. Select the cells that contain the formatting you want to copy.

2. Click the **Format Painter** button on the Standard toolbar. Excel copies the formatting. The mouse pointer changes into a paintbrush with a plus sign next to it.

3. Click one cell or drag over several cells to which you want to apply the copied formatting.

4. Release the mouse button, and Excel copies the formatting and applies it to the selected cells.

**TIP**

**Painting Several Cells**   To paint several areas with the same formatting at one time, double-click the **Format Painter** button to toggle it on. When you're through, press **Esc** or click the **Format Painter** button again to return to a normal mouse pointer.

In this lesson, you learned how to format numbers and to copy formatting from one cell to another. You also learned how to customize your text formatting to achieve the look you want. In the next lesson, you learn how to add borders and shading to the cells in your worksheet.

# LESSON 12
# Adding Cell Borders and Shading

*In this lesson, you learn how to add borders and shading to your worksheets.*

## ADDING BORDERS TO CELLS

As you work with your worksheet onscreen, you'll notice that each cell is identified by gridlines that surround the cell. By default, these gridlines do not print; even if you choose to print them, they don't look very good on the printed page. To create well-defined lines on the printout (and onscreen, for that matter), you can add borders to selected cells or entire cell ranges. A border can appear on all four sides of a cell or only on selected sides; it's up to you.

**TIP**

> **Printing the Gridlines**    It's true that gridlines do not print by default. But if you want to try printing your worksheet with gridlines, just to see what it looks like, open the **File** menu, select **Page Setup**, click the **Sheet** tab, check the **Gridlines** box, and click **OK**.

To add borders to a cell or range, perform the following steps:

1. Select the cell(s) around which you want a border to appear.

2. Open the **Format** menu and choose **Cells**. The Format Cells dialog box appears.

3. Click the **Border** tab to see the Border options shown in Figure 12.1.

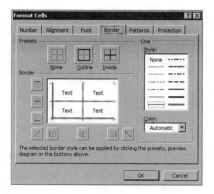

**FIGURE 12.1**
*Choose Border options from the Format Cells dialog box.*

4. Select the desired position, style (thickness), and color for the border. The position of the border is selected using the buttons along the left of the Border box. You also can click inside the **Border** box itself to place the border.

5. Click **OK** or press **Enter**.

When adding borders to a worksheet, hiding the gridlines onscreen gives you a preview of how the borders will look when printed. To hide gridlines, select the **Tools** menu, select **Options** (this opens the Options dialog box), and then select the **View** tab. Remove the check mark from the Gridlines check box, and then click **OK** to return to the worksheet. Selecting this option has no effect on whether the gridlines actually print, only on whether they are displayed onscreen.

**TIP**

> **Add Borders from the Toolbar**   You can use the Borders button on the Formatting toolbar to add a border to cells or cell ranges. Select the cells, and then click the **Borders** drop-down arrow on the Formatting toolbar to select a border type.

## ADDING SHADING TO CELLS

Another way to offset certain cells in a worksheet is to add shading to those cells. With shading, you can add a color or gray shading to the background of a cell. You can add shading that consists of a solid color, or you can select a pattern as part of the shading options, such as a repeating diagonal line.

Follow these steps to add shading to a cell or range. As you make your selections, keep in mind that if you plan to print your worksheet with a black-and-white printer, the colors you select might not provide enough contrast on the printout to provide any differentiation between ranges of cells. You can always use the Print Preview command (as explained in Lesson 16, "Printing Your Workbook") to view your results in black and white before you print.

1. Select the cell(s) you want to shade.

2. Open the **Format** menu and choose **Cells**.

3. Click the **Patterns** tab. Excel displays the shading options (see Figure 12.2).

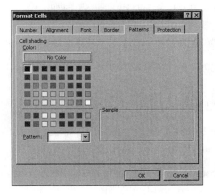

**FIGURE 12.2**
*Choose colors and patterns from the Patterns tab of the Format Cells dialog box.*

4. Click the **Pattern** drop-down arrow to see a grid that contains colors and patterns.

5. Select the shading color and pattern you want to use. The Color options let you choose a color for the overall shading. The Pattern options let you select a black or colored pattern that is placed on top of the cell-shading color you selected. A preview of the results appears in the Sample box.

6. When you have finished making your selections, click **OK**.

**TIP**

**Add Cell Shading with the Toolbar**    Select the cells you want to shade. Click the **Fill Color** drop-down arrow on the Formatting toolbar and then select the fill color from the Color palette that appears.

## Using AutoFormat

If you don't want to take the time to test different border types and shading styles, you can let Excel help you with the task of adding some emphasis and interest to the cells of your worksheet. You can take advantage of AutoFormat, which provides various predesigned table formats that you can apply to a worksheet.

To use predesigned formats, perform the following steps:

1. Select the cell(s) that contain the data you want to format. This could be the entire worksheet.

2. Select the **Format** menu, and then select **AutoFormat**. The AutoFormat dialog box appears (see Figure 12.3).

3. Scroll through the list to view the various AutoFormat styles provided. When you find a format that you want to use, click it to select it.

4. To prevent AutoFormat from overwriting certain existing formatting (such as numbers, alignment, or fonts), click the **Options** button and deselect the appropriate check boxes.

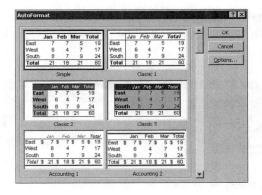

**FIGURE 12.3**
*Select a format from the AutoFormat dialog box.*

5. Click **OK**, and your worksheet is formatted.

TIP

> **Yuck! I Chose That?**    If you don't like what AutoFormat did to your worksheet, click the **Undo** button (or press **Ctrl+Z**).

## APPLYING CONDITIONAL FORMATTING

Another useful formatting feature that Excel provides is conditional formatting. Conditional formatting allows you to specify that certain results in the worksheet be formatted so that they stand out from the other entries in the worksheet. For example, if you wanted to track all the monthly sales figures that are below a certain amount, you can use conditional formatting to format them in red. Conditional formatting formats only cells that meet a certain condition.

To apply conditional formatting, follow these steps:

1. Select the cells to which you want to apply the conditional formatting.

**2.** Select the **Format** menu and select **Conditional Formatting**. The Conditional Formatting dialog box appears, as shown in Figure 12.4.

**FIGURE 12.4**
*Apply formats conditionally to highlight certain values.*

**3.** Be sure that **Cell Value Is** is selected in the Condition 1 drop-down box on the left of the dialog box.

**4.** In the next drop-down box to the right, you select the condition. The default is Between. Other conditions include Equal To, Greater Than, Less Than, and other possibilities. Use the drop-down box to select the appropriate condition.

**5.** After selecting the condition, you must specify a cell or cells in the worksheet that Excel can use as a reference for the conditional formatting. For example, if you select Less Than as the condition, you must specify a cell in the worksheet that contains a value that can be used for comparison with the cells to which you are applying the conditional formatting. Click the **Shrink** button on the Conditional Formatting dialog box. You are returned to the worksheet. Select the reference cell for the condition.

**6.** Click the **Expand** button on the Conditional Formatting dialog box to expand the dialog box.

**7.** Now you can set the formatting that will be applied to cells that meet your condition. Click the **Format** button in the Conditional Formatting dialog box and select the formatting options for your condition in the Format Cells dialog box.

Then click **OK**. Figure 12.5 shows a conditional format that applies bold and italic to values that are less than the value contained in cell D6.

**FIGURE 12.5**
*Set the various options for your conditional formatting.*

8. After setting the conditions to be met for conditional formatting (you can click **Add** to set more than one condition), click **OK**.

You are returned to the worksheet. Cells that meet the condition you set up for conditional formatting will be formatted with the options you specified. Figure 12.6 shows cells that the settings used in Figure 12.5 conditionally formatted.

| | A | B | C | D | E | F | G | H | I | J |
|---|---|---|---|---|---|---|---|---|---|---|
| 1 | | | | | | | | | | |
| 2 | | | | | | | | | | |
| 3 | | | Employee Commissions Week of 03/19/01 | | | | | | | |
| 4 | | | | | | | | | | |
| 5 | | First Name | Last Name | Sales Amount | Commission | | | | | |
| 6 | | Nancy | Davy | $  6,000.00 | $  1,500.00 | | | | | |
| 7 | | Janet | Leverling | $  4,500.00 | *$  1,125.00* | | | | | |
| 8 | | Steven | Buchanan | $  5,000.00 | *$  1,250.00* | | | | | |
| 9 | | Snidley | Backlash | $  7,200.00 | $  1,800.00 | | | | | |
| 10 | | Henry | Cotton | $  6,350.00 | $  1,587.50 | | | | | |
| 11 | | Alice | Smith | $  4,900.00 | *$  1,225.00* | | | | | |
| 12 | | | | | | | | | | |
| 13 | | | | | | | | | | |
| 14 | | | | | | | | | | |
| 15 | | | | | | | | | | |
| 16 | | | | | | | | | | |
| 17 | | | | | | | | | | |
| 18 | | | | | | | | | | |
| 19 | | | | | | | | | | |
| 20 | | | | | | | | | | |
| 21 | | | | | | | | | | |
| 22 | | | | | | | | | | |
| 23 | | | | | | | | | | |

Sheet1 \ Sheet2 / Sheet3 /

**FIGURE 12.6**
*Conditional formatting formats only the cells that meet your conditions.*

**TIP**

> **Conditional Formatting Applied to Formulas** You also can set up conditional formatting to highlight cells that contain a particular formula or function. Select **Formula Is** for Condition 1 in the Conditional Formatting dialog box and then type the formula or function in the box to the right.

In this lesson, you learned some ways to enhance the appearance of your worksheets with borders and shading. In the next lesson, you learn how to work with ranges and create range names.

# LESSON 13

# Working with Ranges

*In this lesson, you learn how to select and name ranges.*

## WHAT IS A RANGE?

When you select a group of cells (which you have done numerous times in the various Excel lessons), you are in fact selecting a range. A cell range can consist of one cell or any group of contiguous cells.

Ranges are referred to by their anchor points (the upper-left corner and the lower-right corner). For example, a range that begins with cell C10 and ends with I14 is referred to as C10:I14.

**PLAIN ENGLISH**

| | |
|---|---|
| **Range** | A group of contiguous cells on an Excel worksheet. |

Although selecting ranges certainly is not rocket science (however, a few tricks for selecting cell ranges are discussed in the next section), you can do several things with a selected range of cells. For example, you can select a range of cells and print them (rather than printing the entire worksheet). You also can name ranges, which makes it much easier to include the cell range in a formula or function (you learn about range names and using range names in formulas later in the lesson).

## SELECTING A RANGE

To select a range using the mouse, follow these steps:

1. Move the mouse pointer to the upper-left corner of a range.

2. Click and hold the left mouse button.

3. Drag the mouse to the lower-right corner of the range and release the mouse button. The cells are highlighted on the worksheet (see Figure 13.1).

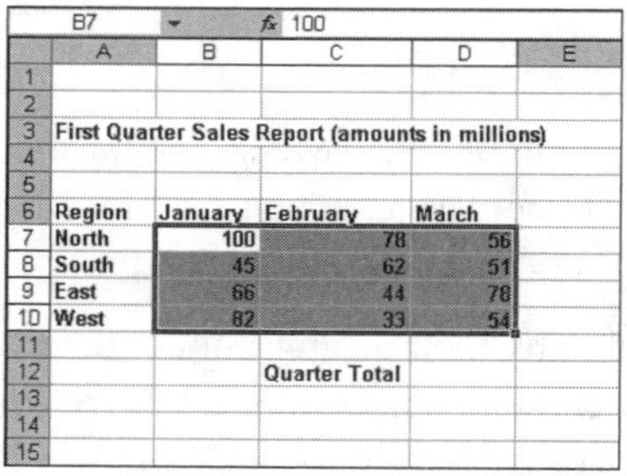

**FIGURE 13.1**
*A range is any combination of cells that forms a rectangle or a square.*

Techniques that you can use to quickly select a row, a column, an entire worksheet, or several ranges are shown in Table 13.1.

**Table 13.1**    Selection Techniques

| To Select This | Do This |
| --- | --- |
| Several ranges | Select the first range, hold down the **Ctrl** key, and select the next range. Continue holding down the **Ctrl** key while you select additional ranges. |
| Row | Click the row heading number at the left edge of the worksheet. You also can press **Shift+Spacebar**. To select several adjacent rows, drag over their headers. To select nonadjacent rows, press **Ctrl** as you click each row's header. |

**Table 13.1**   (continued)

| To Select This | Do This |
| --- | --- |
| Column | Click the column heading letter at the top edge of the worksheet. You also can press **Ctrl+Spacebar**. |
| Entire worksheet | Click the **Select All** button (the blank rectangle in the upper-left corner of the worksheet, above row 1 and left of column A). You also can press **Ctrl+A**. |
| The same range on several sheets | Press and hold **Ctrl** as you click the worksheets you want to use, and then select the range in the usual way. |
| Range that is out of view | Press **Ctrl+G** (**Go To**) or click in the **Name** box on the Formula bar and type the address of the range you want to select. For example, to select the range R100 to T250, type **R100:T250** and press **Enter**. |

**TIP**

**Deselecting a Range**   To deselect a range, click any cell in the worksheet.

Selected cells are not highlighted in reverse video, as in previous versions of Excel, but in a slightly grayed tone, so you still can read your data.

## NAMING RANGES

Up to this point, when you have created formulas or functions or formatted cells in a worksheet, you have specified cells and cell ranges using the cell addresses. You also can name a cell or range of cells. For example, you could select a range of values and assign that range a name. You also could select a range of cells that includes your expenses and name that range EXPENSES. You then can name a range of cells that includes your income and name that range

INCOME. It would be very simple to then create a formula that sub-tracts your expenses from your income using the range names that you created. The formulas would be written as follows:

```
=INCOME-EXPENSES
```

Using range names in formulas and functions definitely can make your life easier. Range names are very useful when you create formu-las or functions that pull information from more than one worksheet in a workbook or different workbooks. You can even use a range name to create a chart (you learn about charts in Lesson 17, "Creating Charts").

Follow these steps to name a range:

1. Select the range you want to name (the cells must be located on the same worksheet). If you want to name a single cell, simply select that cell.

2. Select the **Insert** menu, point at **Name**, and then select **Define**. The Define Name dialog box appears (see Figure 13.2).

**FIGURE 13.2**
*Use the Define Name dialog box to name a cell range.*

3. Type the name for the range in the box at the top of the dia-log box. You can use up to 255 characters, and valid range names can include letters, numbers, periods, and underlines, but no spaces.

4. Click the **Add** button to name the range. The name is added to the list of range names.

5. Click **OK**.

**TIP**

> **Selecting a Different Range**   You can change the selected range from the Define Name dialog box. Click the **Shrink** button at the bottom of the dialog box, and then select the range on the worksheet. To return to the dialog box, click the **Expand** button on the Define Name dialog box.

You also can use the Define Name dialog box to delete any unwanted range names. Select **Insert**, point at **Name**, and then select **Define**. Select an unwanted range name from the list and click the **Delete** button. To close the dialog box, click **OK**.

**TIP**

> **Quickly Create a Range Name**   You also can create a range name by typing it into the Name box on the Formula bar. Select the cell range, click in the Name box, and type the name for the range. Then press **Enter**.

## CREATING RANGE NAMES FROM WORKSHEET LABELS

You also can create range names using the column and row labels that you have created for your worksheet. The row labels are used to create a range name for each row of cells, and the column labels are used to create a range name for each column of cells. Follow these steps:

1. Select the worksheet, including the column and row labels.

2. Select the **Insert** menu, point at **Name**, and then select **Create**. The Create Names dialog box appears (see Figure 13.3).

**FIGURE 13.3**
*Use the Create Names dialog box to create range names for the cells in the worksheet.*

3. Click in the check boxes that define the position of the row and column labels in the worksheet.

4. After specifying the location of the row and column labels, click **OK**.

You can check the range names (and their range of cells) that were created using the Create Name feature in the Define Name dialog box. Select **Insert**, point at **Name**, and then select **Define**. All the range names that you created appear in the Names in Workbook list.

## INSERTING A RANGE NAME INTO A FORMULA OR FUNCTION

As previously discussed in this lesson, range names make it easy for you to specify a range of cells in a formula or function. To insert a range name into a formula or function, follow these steps:

1. Click in the cell where you want to place the formula or function.

2. Type the formula or function (begin the formula or function with the equal sign).

3. When you are ready to insert the range name into the formula or function, select the **Insert** menu, point at **Name**, and select **Paste**. The Paste Name dialog box appears (see Figure 13.4).

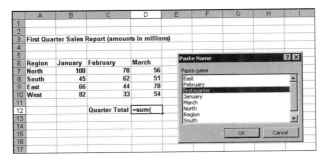

**FIGURE 13.4**
*Use the Paste Name dialog box to insert a range name into a formula or function.*

4. Select the range name you want to place in the formula or function, and then click **OK**.

5. Finish typing the formula or function (including the appropriate operators).

6. Press **Enter** to place the formula or function into the cell and return the calculated value.

In this lesson, you learned how to select and name ranges. You also learned how to insert a range name in a formula or function. In the next lesson, you learn how to manipulate cells, delete and add rows and columns, and work with column widths and row heights.

# LESSON 14

# Inserting and Removing Cells, Rows, and Columns

*In this lesson, you learn how to rearrange the data in your worksheet by adding and removing cells, rows, and columns. You also learn how to adjust the width of your columns and the height of your rows to best use the worksheet space.*

## INSERTING ROWS AND COLUMNS

As you edit and enhance your worksheets, you might need to add rows or columns within the worksheet. Inserting entire rows and columns into your worksheet is very straightforward. Follow these steps:

1. To insert a single row or column, select a cell to the right of where you want to insert a column, or below where you want to insert a row.

   To insert multiple columns or rows, select the number of columns or rows you want to insert. To insert columns, drag over the column letters at the top of the worksheet. To insert rows, drag over the row numbers. For example, select three column letters or row numbers to insert three rows or columns.

2. Select the **Insert** menu, and then select **Rows** or **Columns**. Excel inserts rows above your selection and columns to the left of your selection. The inserted rows or columns contain the same formatting as the cells (or rows and columns) you

selected in step 1. Figure 14.1 shows a worksheet in which additional columns have been added to a worksheet.

| | | | | | | | | | |
|---|---|---|---|---|---|---|---|---|---|
| **Microsoft Excel - customer orders** | | | | | | | | | _ □ × |

File  Edit  View  Insert  Format  Tools  Data  Window  Help

| | A | B | C | D | E | F | G | H | I |
|---|---|---|---|---|---|---|---|---|---|
| 4 | | | | | | | | | |
| 5 | | | | | | | | | |
| 6 | First Name | Last Name | | | | | nt | Start Date | |
| 7 | Nancy | Davy | | | | | m | 1/23/1995 | |
| 8 | Janet | Leverling | | | | | nd | 3/10/1997 | |
| 9 | Steven | Buchanan | | | 225 | Architects | | 5/12/1997 | |
| 10 | Snidley | Backlash | | | 110 | Porches and | | 1/28/1998 | |
| 11 | Henry | Cotton | | | 623 | New | | 7/7/1996 | |
| 12 | Alice | Smith | | | 332 | Porches and | | 5/4/1997 | |
| 13 | Bob | Palooka | | | 234 | Architects | | 9/8/1999 | |
| 14 | Cleo | Katrina | | | 543 | Kitchen | | 4/9/1999 | |
| 15 | Robert | Buchanan | | | 227 | Bathroom | | 8/15/2000 | |
| 16 | Richard | Jones | | | 333 | Kitchen | | 3/10/1999 | |
| 17 | Carmella | Jones | | | 434 | Living Room | | 2/1/2001 | |
| 18 | Amy | Buchanan | | | 654 | Architects | | 3/10/2001 | |
| 19 | | | | | | | | | |
| 20 | | | | | | | | | |
| 21 | | | | | | | | | |
| 22 | | | | | | | | | |
| 23 | | | | | | | | | |
| 24 | | | | | | | | | |
| 25 | | | | | | | | | |
| 26 | | | | | | | | | |

Insert Options menu: Format Same As Left / Format Same As Right / Clear Formatting

Sheet1 / Sheet2 \ Sheet3 /

Ready

**FIGURE 14.1**
*Columns can be inserted easily into an Excel worksheet.*

As you can see, when you insert rows or columns, the Insert Options shortcut icon appears to the right of the inserted columns, or below inserted rows. Use the Insert Options menu to specify from where the column or row should copy its formatting. For example, in the case of inserted columns, you can choose to copy the formatting from the column to the right or left of the inserted column or columns, or you can choose to clear the formatting in the inserted columns.

**TIP**

**Fast Insert**   To quickly insert rows or columns, select one or more rows or columns, right-click one of them, and choose **Insert** from the shortcut menu.

## REMOVING ROWS AND COLUMNS

When you delete a row in your worksheet, the rows below the deleted row move up to fill the space. When you delete a column, the columns to the right shift left.

Follow these steps to delete a row or column:

1. Click the row number or column letter of the row or column you want to delete. You can select more than one row or column by dragging over the row numbers or column letters.

2. Select the **Edit** menu, and then select **Delete**. Excel deletes the rows or columns and renumbers the remaining rows and columns sequentially. All cell references in formulas and functions are updated appropriately.

## INSERTING CELLS

Although inserting rows and columns makes it easy to dramatically change the layout of a worksheet, occasionally you might need to insert only a cell, or cells, into a worksheet. Inserting cells causes the data in existing cells to shift down a row or over a column to create a space for the new cells.

**CAUTION**

**Watch Your Formulas and Functions**   Inserting cells into a worksheet can throw off the cell references in formulas and functions. Double-check your formulas and functions after inserting cells to be sure the calculations are acting on the appropriate cell addresses.

To insert a single cell or a group of cells, follow these steps:

1. Select the area where you want the new cells inserted. Excel inserts the same number of cells as you select.

2. Select the **Insert** menu, and then select **Cells**. The Insert dialog box appears (see Figure 14.2).

**FIGURE 14.2**
*You can insert cells into a worksheet using the Insert dialog box.*

3. Select **Shift Cells Right** or **Shift Cells Down** (or you can choose to have an entire row or column inserted).

4. Click **OK**. Excel inserts the cells and shifts the adjacent cells in the direction you specify.

You will find that inserting cells is useful if you have entered rows of information and have mismatched data, such as a customer's name with someone else's order information. Inserting a couple of cells enables you to quickly edit the data without having to delete data or insert a new row.

**TIP**

**Drag Insert Cells**    A quick way to insert cells is to select the number of cells you want, hold down the **Shift** key, and then drag the fill handle up, down, left, or right to set the position of the new cells.

## REMOVING CELLS

You already learned about deleting the data in cells back in Lesson 10, "Editing Worksheets," and you learned that you also can delete cells from a worksheet. Eliminating cells from the worksheet, rather than just clearing their contents, means that the cells surrounding the deleted cells in the worksheet are moved to fill the gap that is created. Remove cells only if you want the other cells in the worksheet to shift to new positions. Otherwise, just delete the data in the cells or type new data into the cells.

If you want to remove cells from a worksheet, follow these steps:

1. Select the cell or range of cells you want to remove.

2. Open the **Edit** menu and choose **Delete**. The Delete dialog box appears (see Figure 14.3).

**FIGURE 14.3**
*Use the Delete dialog box to specify how the gap left by the deleted cells should be filled.*

3. Select **Shift Cells Left** or **Shift Cells Up** to specify how the remaining cells in the worksheet should move to fill the gap left by the deleted cells.

4. Click **OK**. Surrounding cells shift to fill the gap left by the deleted cells.

As with inserting cells, you should check the cell references in your formulas and functions after removing cells from the worksheet. Be sure that your calculations are referencing the appropriate cells on the worksheet.

# ADJUSTING COLUMN WIDTH AND ROW HEIGHT WITH A MOUSE

When you are working in Excel, it doesn't take long to realize that the default column width of 8.43 characters doesn't accommodate long text entries or values that have been formatted as currency or other numeric formats. You can adjust the width of a column quickly by using the mouse.

You also can adjust row heights using the mouse. However, your row heights will adjust to any font size changes that you make to data held in a particular row. Row heights also adjust if you wrap text entries within them. You probably will find that you need to adjust column widths in your worksheets far more often than row heights.

**CAUTION**

**What Is ########?**   When you format a value in a cell with a numeric formatting, and Excel cannot display the result in the cell because of the column width, Excel places ######## in the cell. This lets you know that you need to adjust the column width so that it can accommodate the entry and its formatting.

To adjust a column width with the mouse, place the mouse pointer on the right border of the column. A sizing tool appears, as shown in Figure 14.4. Drag the column border to the desired width. You also can adjust the column width to automatically accommodate the widest entry within a column; just double-click the sizing tool. This is called AutoFit, and the column adjusts according to the widest entry.

If you want to adjust several columns at once, select the columns. Place the mouse on any of the column borders, and drag to increase or decrease the width. Each selected column is adjusted to the width you select.

Changing row heights is similar to adjusting column widths. Place the mouse on the lower border of a row and drag the sizing tool to increase or decrease the row height. To change the height of multiple rows, select the rows, and then drag the border of any of the selected rows to the desired height.

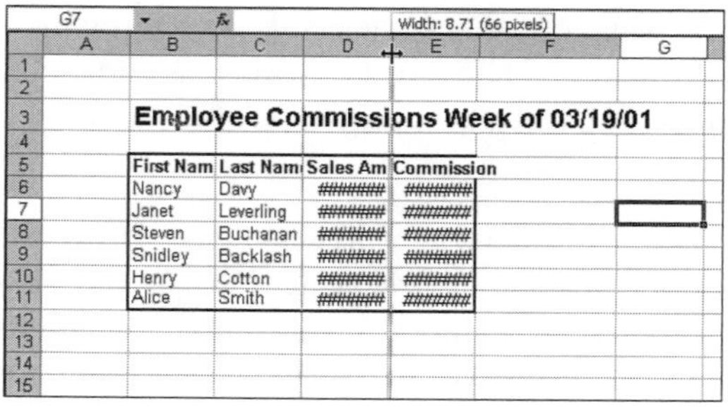

**FIGURE 14.4**
*Use the column width sizing tool to adjust the width of a column.*

## USING THE FORMAT MENU FOR PRECISE CONTROL

If you want to precisely specify the width of a column or columns, or the height of a row or rows, you can enter specific sizes using a dialog box. This provides you with a little more control than just dragging a row height or column width.

To specify a column width, follow these steps:

1. Select the columns you want to change.

2. Select the **Format** menu, point at **Column**, and then select **Width**. The Column Width dialog box appears (see Figure 14.5).

3. Type the column width into the dialog box (the width is measured in number of characters).

4. Click **OK**. Your column(s) width is adjusted accordingly.

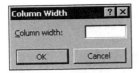

**FIGURE 14.5**
*Column widths also can be specified in the Column Width dialog box.*

Adjusting row heights is similar to adjusting column widths. Select the row or rows, and then select the **Format** menu, point at **Rows**, and select **Height**. In the Row Height dialog box that appears, type in the row height and click **OK**.

In this lesson, you learned how to insert and delete cells, rows, and columns. You also learned how to change row heights and column widths. In the next lesson, you will learn how to select, insert, delete, and move your Excel worksheets.

# LESSON 15
# Managing Your Worksheets

*In this lesson, you learn how to add and delete worksheets within workbooks. You also learn how to copy, move, and rename worksheets.*

## SELECTING WORKSHEETS

By default, each workbook consists of three worksheets whose names appear on tabs at the bottom of the Excel window. You can add or delete worksheets as desired. One advantage of having multiple worksheets within a workbook is that it enables you to organize your data into logical chunks. Another advantage of having separate worksheets for your data is that you easily can reorganize the worksheets (and the associated data) in a workbook.

Before you learn about the details of inserting, deleting, and copying worksheets, you should know how to select one or more worksheets. Selecting a single worksheet is a method of moving from worksheet to worksheet in a workbook.

Selecting multiple worksheets in a workbook, however, is another story. Selecting multiple workbooks enables you to apply the same autoformatting, or cell formatting, to more than one worksheet at a time. This is particularly useful if you have several worksheets in a workbook that will end up looking very much the same. For example, you might have a workbook that contains four worksheets—each of the worksheets serving as a quarterly summary. Because the design of these worksheets is similar, applying formatting to more than one sheet at a time enables you to keep the sheets consistent in appearance.

To select a worksheet or worksheets, perform one of the following actions:

- To select a single worksheet, click its tab. The tab is highlighted to show that the worksheet is selected.

- To select several neighboring or adjacent worksheets, click the tab of the first worksheet in the group, and then hold down the **Shift** key and click the tab of the last worksheet in the group. Each worksheet tab will be highlighted (but only the first sheet selected will be visible).

- To select several nonadjacent worksheets, hold down the **Ctrl** key and click each worksheet's tab.

If you select two or more worksheets, they remain selected as a group until you ungroup them. To ungroup worksheets, do one of the following:

- Right-click one of the selected worksheets and choose **Ungroup Sheets**.

- Hold down the **Shift** key and click the tab of the active worksheet.

- Click any worksheet tab to deselect all the other worksheets.

## INSERTING WORKSHEETS

When you create a new workbook, it contains three worksheets. You easily can add additional worksheets to a workbook.

Follow these steps to add a worksheet to a workbook:

1. Select the worksheet that you want to be to the right of the inserted worksheet. For example, if you select the quarter3

sheet shown in Figure 15.1, the new sheet will be inserted to the left of quarter3.

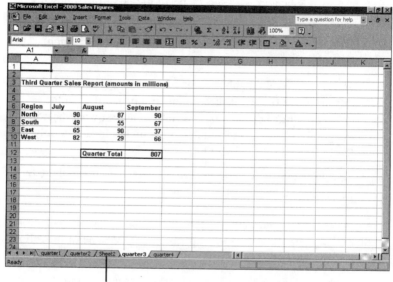

New worksheet

**FIGURE 15.1**
*Excel inserts the new worksheet to the left of the active worksheet.*

2. Select the **Insert** menu.

3. Select **Worksheet**. Excel inserts the new worksheet to the right of the previously selected worksheet.

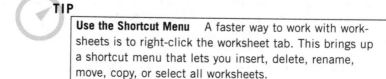

**TIP**

> **Use the Shortcut Menu**   A faster way to work with worksheets is to right-click the worksheet tab. This brings up a shortcut menu that lets you insert, delete, rename, move, copy, or select all worksheets.

**TIP**

> **Start with More Sheets**    You can change the default
> number of worksheets Excel places in a new workbook
> by opening the **Tools** menu, selecting **Options**, clicking
> the **General** tab, and then changing the number in the
> **Sheets in New Workbook** option. Click **OK** to save your
> changes. The maximum value for the number of sheets
> in a workbook is determined by the amount of memory
> on your computer. You might find that using more than
> 20 sheets in a workbook that are full of data start to
> slow down Excel's overall performance.

## DELETING WORKSHEETS

If you find that you have a worksheet you no longer need, or if you
plan to use only one worksheet of the three that Excel puts into each
workbook by default, you can remove the unwanted worksheets.
Here's how you remove a worksheet:

1. Select the worksheets you want to delete.

2. Select the **Edit** menu, and then select **Delete Sheet**.

3. If the sheet contains data, a dialog box appears, asking you to
   confirm the deletion. Click **Delete** to delete the sheet. You
   will lose any data that the sheet contained.

You can delete multiple sheets if you want. Use the techniques discussed earlier in this lesson to select multiple sheets, and then use
steps 2 and 3 in this section to delete the sheets.

## MOVING AND COPYING WORKSHEETS

You can move or copy worksheets within a workbook, or from one
workbook to another. Copying a worksheet enables you to copy the

formatting of the sheet and other items, such as the column labels and the row labels. Follow these steps:

1. Select the worksheet, or worksheets, you want to move or copy. If you want to move or copy worksheets from one workbook to another, be sure the target workbook is open.

2. Select the **Edit** menu and choose **Move or Copy Sheet**. The Move or Copy dialog box appears, as shown in Figure 15.2.

**FIGURE 15.2**
*The Move or Copy dialog box asks where you want to copy or move a worksheet.*

3. To move the worksheets to a different workbook, be sure that workbook is open, and then select that workbook's name from the To Book drop-down list. If you want to move or copy the worksheets to a new workbook, select **(New Book)** in the To Book drop-down list. Excel creates a new workbook and then copies or moves the worksheets to it.

4. In the Before Sheet list box, choose which worksheet you want to follow the selected worksheets.

5. To move the selected worksheet, skip to step 6. To copy the selected worksheets instead of moving them, select the **Create a Copy** option.

6. Select **OK**. The selected worksheets are copied or moved as specified.

## MOVING A WORKSHEET WITHIN A WORKBOOK WITH DRAG AND DROP

A fast way to copy or move worksheets within a workbook is to use drag and drop. First, select the tab of the worksheet(s) you want to copy or move.

Move the mouse pointer over one of the selected tabs, click and hold the mouse button, and drag the tab where you want it moved. To copy the worksheet, hold down the **Ctrl** key while dragging. When you release the mouse button, the worksheet is copied or moved.

## MOVING OR COPYING A WORKSHEET BETWEEN WORKBOOKS WITH DRAG AND DROP

You also can use the Drag-and-Drop feature to quickly copy or move worksheets between workbooks.

1. Open the workbooks you want to use for the copy or move.

2. Select **Window** and then **Arrange**. The Arrange dialog box opens.

3. You can arrange the different workbook windows horizontally, vertically, tiled, or cascaded in the Excel application window. For more than two open workbooks, your best selection is probably the **Tiled** option (see Figure 15.3).

4. After making your selection, click **OK** to arrange the workbook windows within the Excel application window.

5. Select the tab of the worksheet(s) you want to copy or move.

6. Move the mouse pointer over one of the selected tabs, click and hold the mouse button, and drag the tab where you want it moved. To copy the worksheet, hold down the **Ctrl** key while dragging.

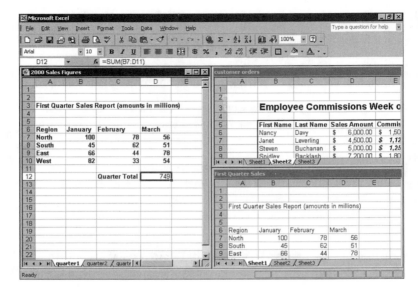

**FIGURE 15.3**
*You can arrange multiple workbooks in the Excel window and then move or copy worksheets.*

7. When you release the mouse button, the worksheet is copied or moved.

## CHANGING WORKSHEET TAB NAMES

By default, all worksheets are named SheetX, where X is a number starting with the number 1. You should change the names that appear on the tabs so you'll have a better idea of the information each sheet contains. Here's how to do it:

1. Double-click the tab of the worksheet you want to rename. The current name is highlighted.

2. Type a new name for the worksheet and press **Enter**. Excel replaces the default name with the name you type.

In this lesson, you learned how to insert, delete, move, copy, and rename worksheets. In the next lesson, you learn how to preview and print your Excel workbooks.

# LESSON 16
# Printing Your Workbook

*In this lesson, you learn how to preview your print jobs, repeat row and column headings on pages, and add headers and footers to your worksheets. You also learn how to print an entire workbook and large worksheets.*

## PREVIEWING A PRINT JOB

After you've finished a particular worksheet and want to send it to the printer, you might want to take a quick look at how the worksheet will look on the printed page. You will find that worksheets don't always print the way they look on the screen.

 To preview a print job, select the **File** menu, and then select **Print Preview**, or click the **Print Preview** button on the Standard toolbar. Your workbook appears in the same format in which it will appear when sent to the printer (see Figure 16.1).

> **LEAD IN HERE**
>
> **A Close-Up View**   Zoom in on any area of the preview by clicking it with the mouse pointer (which looks like a magnifying glass). Or, use the **Zoom** button on the Print Preview toolbar.

When you have finished previewing your worksheet, you can print the worksheet by clicking the **Print** button, or you can return to the worksheet by clicking **Close**.

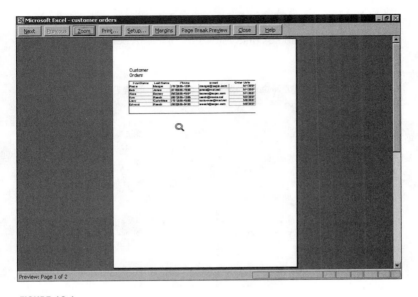

**FIGURE 16.1**
*By previewing the worksheet, you can determine which page layout attributes need adjusting.*

## CHANGING THE PAGE SETUP

After you preview your worksheet, you might want to adjust page attributes, or change the way the page is set up for printing. For example, you might want to print the column and row labels on every page of the printout. This is particularly useful for large worksheets that span several pages; then, you don't have to keep looking back to the first page of the printout to determine what the column headings are.

Printing column and row labels and other worksheet page attributes, such as scaling a worksheet to print out on a single page or adding headers or footers to a worksheet printout, are handled in the Page Setup dialog box. To access this dialog box, select the **File** menu and select **Page Setup** (see Figure 16.2).

The following sections provide information on some of the most common page setup attributes that you will work with before printing your Excel worksheets.

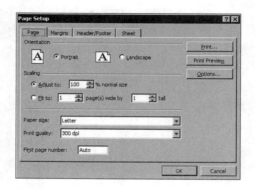

**FIGURE 16.2**
*Access the Page Setup dialog box to be sure your worksheet page is set to print correctly.*

## PRINTING COLUMN AND ROW LABELS ON EVERY PAGE

Excel provides a way for you to select labels and titles that are located on the top edge and left side of a large worksheet and to print them on every page of the printout. This option is useful when a worksheet is too wide to print on a single page. If you don't use this option, the extra columns or rows are printed on subsequent pages without any descriptive labels.

Follow these steps to print column or row labels on every page:

1. Select the **File** menu, and then select **Page Setup**. The Page Setup dialog box appears.

2. Click the **Sheet** tab to display the Sheet options (see Figure 16.3).

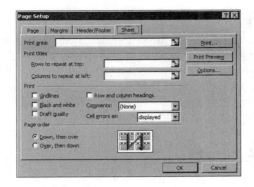

**FIGURE 16.3**
*Use the Sheet tab to specify headings you want to repeat in the printout.*

3. To repeat column labels and a worksheet title, click the **Shrink** button to the right of the Rows to Repeat at Top text box.

4. Drag over the rows that you want to print on every page. A dashed line border surrounds the selected area, and absolute cell references with dollar signs ($) appear in the Rows to Repeat at Top text box.

5. Click the **Expand** button on the collapsed dialog box to expand the Page Setup dialog box.

6. To repeat row labels that appear on the left of the worksheet, click the **Shrink** button to the right of the Columns to Repeat at Left text box. Excel reduces the Page Setup dialog box.

7. Select the columns that contain the row labels you want to repeat.

8. Click the **Expand** button to return again to the Page Setup dialog box.

9. To print your worksheet, click **Print** to display the Print dialog box. Then click **OK**.

**NOTE**

> **Select Your Print Area Carefully**    If you select rows or columns to repeat, and those rows or columns are part of your print area, the selected rows or columns might print twice. To fix this, select your print area again, leaving out the rows or columns you're repeating.

**LEAD IN HERE**

> **Access Print Preview from Other Dialog Boxes**    Page Setup and Print dialog boxes also include a Preview button, so you can check any last-minute changes you made in either dialog box without having to close the box first.

## SCALING A WORKSHEET TO FIT ON A PAGE

If your worksheet is too large to print on one page even after you change the orientation and margins, consider using the **Fit To** option. This option shrinks the worksheet to make it fit on the specified number of pages. You can specify the document's width and height.

Follow these steps to scale a worksheet to fit on a page:

1. Select the **File** menu, and then select **Page Setup**. The Page Setup dialog box appears.

2. Click the **Page** tab to display the Page options.

3. In the Fit to XX Page(s) Wide by XX Tall text boxes, enter the number of pages into which you want Excel to fit your data.

4. Click **OK** to close the Page Setup dialog box and return to your worksheet, or click the **Print** button in the Page Setup dialog box to display the Print dialog box, and then click **OK** to print your worksheet.

**TIP**

**Change the Page Orientation**    The Page tab of the Page
Setup dialog box also enables you to change the orientation of the worksheet from Portrait to Landscape.
Landscape orientation is useful if you have a worksheet
with a large number of columns.

## ADDING HEADERS AND FOOTERS

Excel enables you to add headers and footers to your worksheets that
will appear at the top and bottom of every page of the printout
(respectively). The information can include any text, as well as page
numbers, the current date and time, the workbook filename, and the
worksheet tab name.

You can choose the headers and footers suggested by Excel, or you
can include any text plus special commands to control the appearance
of the header or footer. For example, you can apply bold, italic, or
underline to the header or footer text. You also can left-align, center,
or right-align your text in a header or footer (see Lesson 11,
"Changing How Numbers and Text Look," for more information).

To add headers and footers, follow these steps:

1. Select the **File** menu, and then select **Page Setup**. The Page
   Setup dialog box appears. Click the **Header/Footer** tab on
   the dialog box (see Figure 16.4).

2. To select a header, click the **Header** drop-down arrow. Excel
   displays a list of suggested header information. Scroll
   through the list and click a header you want. The sample
   header appears at the top of the Header/Footer tab.

**TIP**

**Don't See One You Like?**    If none of the suggested headers or footers suit you, click the **Custom Header** or **Custom
Footer** button and enter your own information.

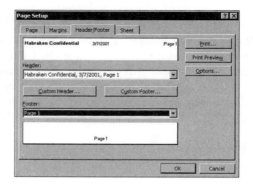

**FIGURE 16.4**
*Add headers and footers with Header/Footer options.*

3. To select a footer, click the **Footer** drop-down arrow. Excel displays a list of suggested footer information. Scroll through the list and click a footer you want. The sample footer appears at the bottom of the Header/Footer tab.

4. Click **OK** to close the Page Setup dialog box and return to your worksheet, or click the **Print** button to display the Print dialog box and click **OK** to print your worksheet.

**TIP**

> **Don't Want Headers or Footers Anymore?** To remove the header and/or footer, choose **(None)** in the **Header** and/or **Footer** lists.

## Printing Your Workbook

After adjusting the page settings for the worksheet and previewing your data, it is time to print. You can print selected data, selected sheets, or the entire workbook.

To print your workbook, follow these steps:

1. If you want to print a portion of the worksheet, select the
   range of cells you want to print. To print only a chart, click it
   (you learn about creating charts in Lesson 17, "Creating
   Charts"). If you want to print one or more worksheets within
   the workbook, select the sheet tabs (see Lesson 15,
   "Managing Your Worksheets"). To print the entire workbook,
   skip this step.

2. Select the **File** menu, and then select **Print** (or press **Ctrl+P**).
   The Print dialog box appears, as shown in Figure 16.5.

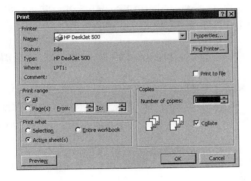

**FIGURE 16.5**
*In the Print dialog box, select your printer and a page range to print.*

 **TIP**

> **Print Using the Default Settings**   If you click the **Print**
> button (instead of using the **File** menu and clicking
> **Print**), Excel prints your current worksheet without letting
> you make any selections.

3. Select the options you would like to use:

   - **Print Range**—Lets you print one or more pages. For
     example, if the selected print area contains 15 pages

and you want to print only pages 5–10, select **Page(s)**, and then type the numbers of the first and last page you want to print into the **From** and **To** boxes.

- **Print What**—Enables you to print the currently selected cells, the selected worksheets, or the entire workbook.

- **Copies**—Enables you to print more than one copy of the selection, worksheet, or workbook.

- **Collate**—Enables you to print a complete copy of the selection, worksheet, or workbook before the first page of the next copy is printed. This option is available when you print multiple copies.

4. Click **OK** to print your selection, worksheet, or workbook.

While your job is printing, you can continue working in Excel. If the printer is working on another job that you (or someone else, in the case of a network printer) sent, Windows holds the job until the printer is ready for it.

Sometimes, you might want to delete a job while it is printing or before it prints. For example, suppose you think of other numbers to add to the worksheet or realize that you forgot to format some text; you'll want to fix these things before you print the file. To display the print queue and delete a print job, follow these steps:

1. Double-click the **Printer** icon in the Windows system tray (at the far right of the taskbar), and the print queue appears.

2. Click the job you want to delete.

3. Select the **Document** menu, and then select **Cancel Printing**, or just press **Delete**.

   To delete all the files from the print queue, open the **Printer** menu and select **Purge Print Documents**. This cancels the print jobs but doesn't delete the files from your computer.

## SELECTING A LARGE WORKSHEET PRINT AREA

You do not always have to print an entire worksheet; instead, you easily can tell Excel what part of the worksheet you want to print by selecting the print area yourself. If the area you select is too large to fit on one page, no problem; Excel breaks it into multiple pages. When you do not select a print area yourself, Excel prints either the entire worksheet or the entire workbook, depending on the options set in the Print dialog box.

To select a print area, follow these steps:

1. Click the upper-left cell of the range you want to print.

2. Drag downward and to the right until the range you want is selected.

3. Select the **File** menu, point at **Print Area**, and then select **Set Print Area**.

To remove the print area so you can print the entire worksheet again, select the **File** menu, select **Print Area**, and select **Clear Print Area**.

## ADJUSTING PAGE BREAKS

When you print a workbook, Excel determines the page breaks based on the paper size, the margins, and the selected print area. To make the pages look better and to break information in logical places, you might want to override the automatic page breaks with your own breaks. However, before you add page breaks, try these options:

- Adjust the widths of individual columns to best use the space.

- Consider printing the workbook using the Landscape orientation.

- Change the left, right, top, and bottom margins to smaller values.

After trying these options, if you still want to insert page breaks, Excel offers you an option of previewing exactly where the page breaks appear, and then adjusting them. Follow these steps:

1. Select the **View** menu and select **Page Break Preview**.

2. If a message appears telling you how to adjust page breaks, click **OK**. Your worksheet is displayed with page breaks, as shown in Figure 16.6.

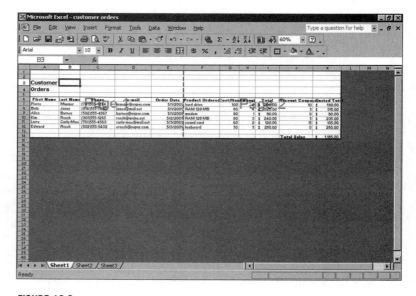

**FIGURE 16.6**
*Check your page breaks before printing your worksheet.*

3. To move a page break, drag the blue line to the desired location.

   To delete a page break, drag it off the screen.

   To insert a page break, move to the first cell in the column to the right of where you want the page break inserted, or move to the row below where you want the break inserted. For example, to insert a page break between columns G and H, move to cell H1. To insert a page break between rows 24 and 25, move to cell A25. Then, open the **Insert** menu and select **Page Break**. A dashed line appears to the left of the selected column or above the selected row.

4. To exit Page Break Preview and return to your normal worksheet view, open the **View** menu and select **Normal**.

In this lesson, you learned how to print all or part of your workbook, as well as how to print a large worksheet. You also learned to adjust page setup attributes, such as column and row labels and headers and footers. In the next lesson, you learn how to create Excel charts.

# LESSON 17
# Creating Charts

*In this lesson, you learn how to create graphical representations (charts) of workbook data.*

## UNDERSTANDING CHARTING TERMINOLOGY

Charts enable you to create a graphical representation of data in a worksheet. You can use charts to make data more understandable to people who view your printed worksheets. Before you start creating charts, you should familiarize yourself with the following terminology:

- **Data Series**—The bars, pie wedges, lines, or other elements that represent plotted values in a chart. For example, a chart might show a set of similar bars that reflects a series of values for the same item. The bars in the same data series all would have the same pattern. If you had more than one pattern of bars, each pattern would represent a separate data series. For example, charting the sales for Territory 1 versus Territory 2 would require two data series—one for each territory. Often, data series correspond to rows of data in your worksheet (although they can correspond to columns of data if that is how you have arranged the information in your worksheet).

- **Categories**—Categories reflect the number of elements in a series. You might have two data series that compare the sales of two territories and four categories that compare these sales over four quarters. Some charts have only one category, and others have several. Categories normally correspond to the columns in your worksheet, with the category labels coming from the column headings.

- **Axis**—One side of a chart. A two-dimensional chart has an x-axis (horizontal) and a y-axis (vertical). The x-axis contains the data series and categories in the chart. If you have more than one category, the x-axis often contains labels that define what each category represents. The y-axis reflects the values of the bars, lines, or plot points. In a three-dimensional chart, the z-axis represents the vertical plane, and the x-axis (distance) and y-axis (width) represent the two sides on the floor of the chart.

- **Legend**—Defines the separate series of a chart. For example, the legend for a pie chart shows what each piece of the pie represents.

- **Gridlines**—Typically, gridlines appear along the y-axis of the chart. The y-axis is where your values are displayed, although they can emanate from the x-axis as well (the x-axis is where label information normally appears on the chart). Gridlines help you determine a point's exact value.

## WORKING WITH DIFFERENT CHART TYPES

With Excel, you can create many types of charts. Some common chart types appear in Figure 17.1. The chart type you choose depends on the kind of data you're trying to chart and how you want to present that data. The following are the major chart types and their purposes:

- **Pie**—Use this chart type to show the relationship among parts of a whole.

- **Bar**—Use this chart type to compare values at a given point in time.

- **Column**—Similar to the bar chart. Use this chart type to emphasize the difference between items.

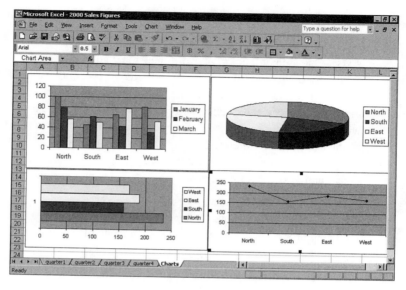

**FIGURE 17.1**
*Excel chart types enable you to analyze and present your data.*

- **Line**—Use this chart type to emphasize trends and the change of values over time.

- **Scatter**—Similar to a line chart. Use this chart type to emphasize the difference between two sets of values.

- **Area**—Similar to the line chart. Use this chart type to emphasize the amount of change in values over time.

Most of these basic chart types also come in three-dimensional varieties. In addition to looking more professional than the standard flat charts, 3D charts often can help your audience distinguish between different sets of data.

## CREATING AND SAVING A CHART

You can place your new chart on the same worksheet that contains the chart data (an embedded chart) or on a separate worksheet (a chart sheet). If you create an embedded chart, it typically is printed side by side with your worksheet data. Embedded charts are useful for showing the actual data and its graphical representation side by side. If you create a chart on a separate worksheet, however, you can print it independently. Both types of charts are linked to the worksheet data that they represent, so when you change the data, the chart is updated automatically.

The **Chart Wizard** button on the Standard toolbar enables you to quickly create a chart. To use the Chart Wizard, follow these steps:

1. Select the data you want to chart. If you typed column or row labels (such as Qtr 1, Qtr 2, and so on) that you want included in the chart, be sure you select those, too.

2. Click the **Chart Wizard** button on the Standard toolbar.

3. The **Chart Wizard - Step 1 of 4** dialog box appears (see Figure 17.2). Select a **Chart Type** and a **Chart Sub-Type** (a variation on the selected chart type). Click **Next**.

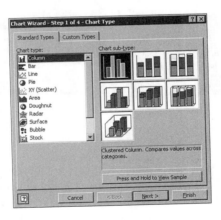

**FIGURE 17.2**
*Choose the chart type using the Chart Wizard.*

4. Next, Excel asks whether the selected range is correct. You can correct the range by typing a new range or by clicking

the **Shrink** button (located at the right end of the **Data Range** text box) and selecting the range you want to use.

5. By default, Excel assumes that your different data series are stored in rows. You can change this to columns, if necessary, by clicking the **Series in Columns** option. When you're ready for the next step, click **Next**.

6. Click the various tabs to change options for your chart (see Figure 17.3). For example, you can delete the legend by clicking the **Legend** tab and deselecting **Show Legend**. You can add a chart title on the **Titles** tab. Add data labels (labels that display the actual value being represented by each bar, line, and so on) by clicking the **Data Labels** tab. When you finish making changes, click **Next**.

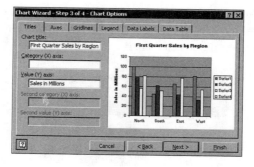

**FIGURE 17.3**
*Select from various chart appearance options.*

7. Finally, Excel asks whether you want to embed the chart (as an object) in the current worksheet (or any other existing worksheet in the workbook) or if you want to create a new worksheet for it. Make your selection and click the **Finish** button. Your completed chart appears.

**TIP**

**Create a Chart Fast!**   To create a chart quickly, select the data you want to use and press **F11**. Excel creates a column chart (the default chart type) on its own sheet. You then can customize the chart as needed.

The charts you create are part of the current workbook. To save a chart, simply save the workbook that contains the chart.

## MOVING AND RESIZING A CHART

To move an embedded chart, click anywhere in the chart area and drag it to the new location. To change the size of a chart, select the chart and drag one of its handles (the black squares that border the chart). Drag a corner handle to change the height and width, or drag a side handle to change only one dimension. (Note that you can't really resize a chart that is on a sheet by itself.)

## PRINTING A CHART

If a chart is an embedded chart, it will print when you print the work-sheet that contains the chart. If you want to print just the embedded chart, click it to select it, and then open the **File** menu and select **Print**. Be sure the **Selected Chart** option is turned on. Then, click **OK** to print the chart.

If you created a chart on a separate worksheet, you can print the chart separately by printing only that worksheet. For more information about printing, refer to Lesson 16, "Printing Your Workbook."

In this lesson, you learned about the different chart types and how to create them. You also learned how to save and print charts. In the next lesson, you will learn to enhance your Excel charts.

# LESSON 18

# Making Your Charts Look Better

*In this lesson, you learn how to enhance your charts using the Chart toolbar and how to add titles, axis titles, and legends to a chart. You also learn how to manipulate text and colors on the chart.*

## SELECTING A CHART OBJECT

A chart is made up of several parts, or objects. For example, a chart can have a title, a legend, and different data series (data series appear on the y-axis, x-axis, or additional axes). To enhance these items on your chart, you first must select the item you want to fix up. To do this, simply click that part or select it from the Chart Objects box on the Chart toolbar (see the next section for help with the toolbar). When a part, such as the legend, is selected, handles (tiny black squares) appear around it, as shown in Figure 18.1.

**TIP**

> **Object**   Any one of the single items found on a chart, such as the legend or title.

When a chart object is selected, you can drag it to a new location. To resize an object, select it and drag one of its handles out to make the object larger, or drag it in to make it smaller. You actually can resize the whole chart by selecting it first and then dragging one of its handles.

Handles

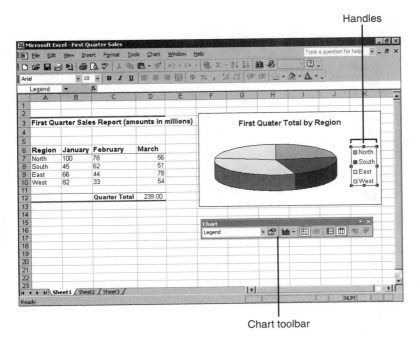

Chart toolbar

**FIGURE 18.1**
*When a chart part is selected, it's surrounded by handles.*

## THE CHART TOOLBAR

You can use the Chart toolbar to quickly change chart attributes. Normally, the Chart toolbar is displayed whenever you select a chart object. If you don't see the Chart toolbar when the chart or any chart object is selected, select the **View** menu, select **Toolbars**, and then select **Chart**.

Table 18.1 describes each button on the **Chart** toolbar.

**Table 18.1** Chart Toolbar Buttons

| Button | Name | Use |
|--------|------|-----|
| Legend ▾ | Chart Objects | Use this pull-down list to quickly select a particular object on the chart. |
| | Format Object | This button opens the format dialog box for the currently selected chart object. |
| | Chart Type | Use this pull-down menu to quickly change the type of chart. |
| | Legend | Use this button to display or hide the legend for the chart. |
| | Data Table | This button enables you to add a table of data to the chart or an axes that coincides with the data used to create the chart or that particular axis. |
| | By Row | Data used for the chart is held in your worksheet in either a row or a column. If the chart doesn't look correct, click this button to switch how the data is read from the worksheet (by row rather than by column) . |

**Table 18.1**    (continued)

| Button | Name | Use |
|--------|------|-----|
|  | By Column | Use this button to switch how the data is read from the work-sheet. This button is used when data is arranged in columns. |
| | Angle Text | Use this button to angle Clockwise text in a title or label soit reads from bottom to top. |
| | Angle Text | Use this button to angle ounterclockwise text in a title or label so it reads from top to bottom. |

## CHANGING THE CHART TYPE

After you create your chart, you might find that a different chart type would be better suited for the type of data that you have in the work-sheet that was used to create the chart. To quickly change the chart type:

1. Click the chart to select it, or choose **Chart Area** from the Chart Objects drop-down list on the Chart toolbar. Selection handles will appear around the entire chart.

   Legend

2. Click the **Chart Type** button drop-down arrow and select another chart type.

**TIP**

> **The Chart I Want Isn't Displayed!**    To change to a chart type that is not on the list, select the **Chart** menu, and then select **Chart Type**. The Chart Type dialog box opens. Choose the new chart type from the list provided.

## ADDING A TITLE AND A LEGEND

Charts provide a great way to take numerical data and display it in a "picture" format that most people can readily understand. However, a title and legend will add clarity to your charts. The title tells you what the chart is about, and legends are particularly useful because they provide color coding of the different data ranges in the chart.

You also can add axis titles that appear along the x- and y-axes (and the z-axis, if the chart is a 3-D chart). These titles provide additional explanatory information related to the different chart axes. Follow these steps:

1. Click the chart to select it, or choose **Chart Area** from the Chart Objects drop-down list on the Chart toolbar. Selection handles appear around the chart area.

2. Select the **Chart** menu, and then select **Chart Options**. The Chart Options dialog box appears.

3. Click the **Titles** tab (see Figure 18.2). Add a chart title and the different axes titles as needed. A sample chart is provided on the right to show you how your changes will look.

4. If you did not include a legend for the chart when you created the chart (as detailed in Lesson 17), click the **Legend** tab, and then click the **Show Legend** check box to select it. Use the different option buttons in the Placement box of the Legend tab to place the legend on the chart.

5. Click **OK** to close the dialog box and return to the chart.

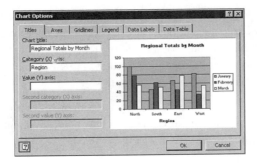

**FIGURE 18.2**
*You can add axes titles to the chart.*

## FORMATTING CHART TEXT, COLORS, AND ALIGNMENT

Because the various text elements on a chart, such as the title or an axis title, are housed in their own text boxes, you can change the formatting for a particular object's text, including the color and alignment, by double-clicking that object. For example, if you double-click the chart title, the Format Chart Title dialog box opens, as shown in Figure 18.3.

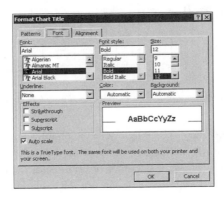

**FIGURE 18.3**
*Double-click any text object in the chart to open its Format dialog box.*

The Format dialog box for a particular chart object provides different tabs you can use to enhance the various elements of that object, such as the text font, borders and colors, and the text alignment. The following list describes each tab on the Format dialog box that you will run into when formatting various chart titles:

- **Font tab**—The Font tab enables you to change the font type and size, and add font attributes, such as bold, italic, and underline, to the text (refer to Figure 18.3).

- **Patterns tab**—The Patterns tab enables you to place a border around the text and select different fill colors for the box that surrounds the particular chart object. You can select the line type and fill color, and even place a shadow on the object's text box (see Figure 18.4).

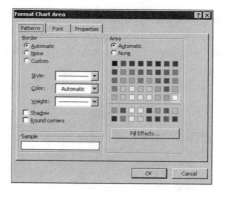

**FIGURE 18.4**
*You can use the Patterns tab to add borders and fill colors to the chart object.*

- **Alignment tab**—The Alignment tab enables you to control both the horizontal alignment (such as center or left) and vertical alignment (such as center or bottom) of the text in the chart object's text box. You can use the Orientation box on this tab to rotate the text in the box. Just drag the text alignment handle in the Orientation box to rotate the text.

When you have finished changing the attributes for a particular chart object text box, click the **OK** button in the dialog box. You will return to your worksheet, and the chart will display the enhancements that you selected.

**LEAD IN HERE**

> **Legends Have a Placement Tab**    Because legends provide color coding of the different data ranges in the chart, they do not include an Alignment tab as the other text object types do. The Format Legend dialog box includes a Placement tab that is used to place the legend on the chart area.

## ENHANCING THE CHART AREA

Another way to enhance the overall look of your Excel chart is to change the color and pattern attributes of the chart area. This is the entire area enclosed within the chart's frame. To enhance the chart area, follow these steps:

1. Select the chart area (click on the chart or select **Chart Area** in the Chart Objects drop-down list on the Chart toolbar).

2. Click the **Format Chart Area** button on the Chart toolbar (or Select **Format, Selected Chart Area**).

3. To change the border and fill color for the entire chart, click the **Patterns** tab and use the drop-down lists and option buttons to select the line weight and color for the chart area.

4. To change the fonts used in the chart area, click the **Font** tab and make the appropriate selections.

5. When you have finished changing the various attributes of the chart area, click the **OK** button to close the dialog box.

In this lesson, you learned how to enhance your Excel charts. In the next lesson, you will learn how to save Excel worksheets for use on the World Wide Web.

# LESSON 19
# Adding Graphics and Other Objects to Worksheets

*In this lesson, you learn how to add clip art and other images to your worksheets.*

## INSERTING CLIP ART INTO A WORKSHEET

Adding clip art or a picture to your worksheet is just a matter of identifying the place in the worksheet where you want to place the picture, and then selecting and inserting a specific picture file. Excel provides a large clip-art library, and you also can place images into your worksheets that you find on the World Wide Web, that you receive attached to e-mail messages, and that are imported from a scanner or digital camera.

Excel embraces several graphic file formats, including the following file types:

- CompuServe GIF (.gif)

- Encapsulated PostScript (.eps)

- Various paint programs (.pcx)

- Tagged Image File format (.tif)

- Windows bitmap (.bmp)

- JPEG file interchange format (.jpg)

- WordPerfect graphics (.wpg)

To insert an image from the Excel clip-art library, follow these steps:

1. Click in the worksheet cell where you would like to place the clip-art image.

2. Select **Insert**, **Picture**, and then select **Clip Art** on the cascading menu. The Insert Clip Art task pane appears (see Figure 19.1).

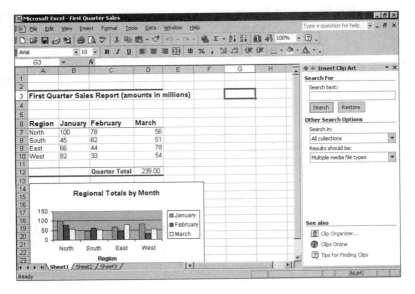

**FIGURE 19.1**
*The Insert Clip Art task pane gives you access to the Excel clip-art gallery.*

3. Type a clip-art theme, such as **animals**, into the **Search Text** area.

4. (Optional) If you want to preclude certain file types from the search to speed up the search process, select the **All Media File Types** drop-down box and deselect any of the file types (ClipArt, Photographs, and so on) as required.

**TIP**

> **Sound and Action Imagery Available, Too**    You can insert sound or movie clips into your worksheets from the Clip Art task pane. By default, they are included in the results for any search you conduct of the entire clip-art gallery.

5.  Click the **Search** button, and various clip-art images that fit your search criteria appear.

6.  When you have located the clip art you want to place in the worksheet, click the image. An image drop-down box appears (see Figure 19.2). Select **Insert** to place the image in your worksheet.

**FIGURE 19.2**
*Click a particular clip-art image to insert it into the worksheet.*

If used appropriately, pictures and clip art definitely can improve the look and feel of your worksheets, particularly if you want to add a company logo to your worksheet. If you find the clip-art library does-n't have what you need, click the **Media Gallery Online** link under the **See Also** section near the bottom of the task pane. Your Web browser opens, and you go to Microsoft's online clip-art library, which offers additional clip-art images for your use.

**TIP**

> **Add a Graphic with Copy and Paste**    You can copy a graphic to the Windows Clipboard from any Windows graphic program that you are running, and then paste it into your Excel worksheet.

## SIZING AND MOVING A PICTURE

To size a graphic, click it to select it. Sizing handles (small circles) appear on the border of the image (see Figure 19.3). Place the mouse on any of these sizing handles. The mouse pointer becomes a sizing tool with arrows pointing in the directions in which you can change the size. Drag to size the graphic. To maintain the height/width ratio of the image so you don't stretch or distort the image, use the sizing han-dles on the corners of the image, and drag diagonally.

**FIGURE 19.3**
*Use the sizing handles to change the size of the image.*

To move the image to a new location in the worksheet, select the image and use the mouse to drag it to a new location. You can place it anywhere some whitespace appears on your worksheet.

Excel 2002 also makes it easy for you to rotate a graphic. Select the image, and then place the mouse pointer on the rotation handle that appears at the top of the graphic (it has a small green handle on the top). Rotate the handle in any direction to rotate the image.

## INSERTING OTHER IMAGE FILE TYPES

As already mentioned, you can add images to your Excel files that you find on the Web, or that you have created using a scanner or digital camera. This enables you to place company logos and even employee pictures on an Excel worksheet. Pictures (other than clip-art files) are inserted using the Insert menu.

Follow these steps to add a picture file to an Excel worksheet:

1. Click in the cell where you want to place the picture.

2. Select **Insert**, **Picture**, and then select **From File** on the cascading menu. The Insert Picture dialog box appears.

3. Use the **Look In** box to locate the drive and folder that contains the picture file. After you locate the picture, click the file to view a preview (see Figure 19.4).

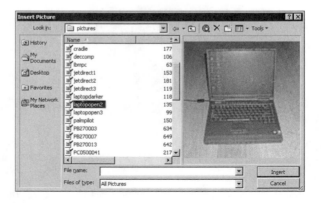

**FIGURE 19.4**
*You can preview your graphical images before inserting them into your worksheet.*

4. After you select the picture you want to insert, click **Insert** in the lower-right corner of the Insert Picture dialog box.

The picture is placed in your worksheet, and the Picture toolbar appears in the worksheet window. The next section provides information on using the Picture toolbar.

> **TIP**
>
> **Deleting Unwanted Images**   Select the picture and press the **Delete** key. The image is removed from the worksheet.

## USING THE PICTURE TOOLBAR

The Picture toolbar provides several tools you can use to modify and edit the images inserted into your worksheets (including clip art). If you don't see the Picture toolbar when an image is selected, right-click on any toolbar and select **Picture**.

Table 19.1 provides a listing and a description of the most commonly used buttons on the Picture toolbar.

**Table 19.1**   The Picture Toolbar Buttons and Their Purposes

| Button | Click To |
| --- | --- |
|  | Insert a new picture at the current picture position. |
| | Change the color of the image to grayscale or black and white. |
| | Crop the image (after selecting, you must drag the image border to a new cropping position). |
| | Rotate the image to the left (counter-clockwise). |
| | Select a line style for the image border (you first must use the Borders and Shading command to add a border to the image). |

**Table 19.1** (continued)

| Button | Click To |
|---|---|
| 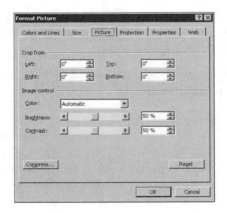 | Open the Format Picture dialog box. |
| | Reset the image to its original formatting values. |

To use one of the tools, select the image (if it is not already selected), and then select the appropriate button on the Picture toolbar. You can select from several formatting options for your picture when you select the **Format Picture** button; this opens the Format Picture dialog box. This dialog box provides tabs such as Color and Lines, Size, and Picture. For example, on the Picture tab, you can adjust the cropping and the brightness and contrast of the image (see Figure 19.5).

**FIGURE 19.5**
*The Format Picture dialog box provides you with access to all the attributes of the selected image.*

When you have finished working in the Format Picture dialog box, click OK. This closes the dialog box and returns you to your worksheet.

**TIP**

> **Cropping a Picture with the Mouse**    Select the picture, and then drag the resizing handles while you hold down the **Shift** key. This will crop the picture rather than resize it.

## DRAWING YOUR OWN PICTURES

You can add additional graphic objects to your worksheets using the Drawing toolbar. This toolbar provides several tools, including line, arrow, rectangle, oval, and text box tools. You also can use the appropriate tools to change the fill color on a box or circle, change the line color on your drawing object, or change the arrow style on arrows you have placed on the worksheet.

To display the Drawing toolbar, select **View**, point at **Toolbar**, and then select **Drawing** from the toolbar list. The Drawing toolbar appears just above the Status bar at the bottom of the Excel window (see Figure 19.6).

**TIP**

> **Quickly Access Toolbars**    You also can right-click any toolbar in the Word window to access the toolbar list; then select **Drawing**.

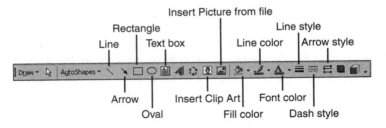

**FIGURE 19.6**
*Use the Drawing toolbar to add graphical elements to your worksheets.*

To draw a particular object, click the appropriate button on the toolbar. Then, drag the mouse to create the object on your worksheet. To draw a square or circle, click the **Rectangle** tool or the **Oval** tool and hold down the **Shift** key as you draw the object with the mouse. If you find that you aren't very good at actually drawing graphical objects, click the **AutoShapes** drop-down arrow (near the left side of the drawing toolbar) and select a particular object shape from the list provided.

You can control the various attributes for a particular object you've drawn. You first must select the object using the selection pointer (click the **Select Objects** tool, and then click the object). You can manipulate the object's line style, fill color, and line color. Just choose the appropriate tool on the toolbar, and make your selection from the list of possibilities.

You also can size and move objects that you draw. Select an object, and use the sizing handles to increase or decrease the size of the particular object. If you want to move the object to a new position, place the mouse pointer in the middle of the selected object and drag it to a new position.

If you draw several related objects, you can select all the objects at once and drag them together to a new location. Select the first object, and then hold down the **Shift** key and select subsequent objects as needed. When you drag any of the objects to a new location, all the selected objects move together.

At times, you will want to delete a particular object from your worksheet. Simply select the object and press **Delete** to remove it.

You will find that the Drawing toolbar provides you with all the tools (except natural artistic ability) you need to create fairly sophisticated custom images. A little practice with the various tools goes a long way in helping you create objects that add interest to your Excel worksheets and charts.

In this lesson, you learned how to add clip art, pictures, and drawing objects to your worksheets. In the next lesson, you will learn how to save an Excel worksheet for use on the Web.

# LESSON 20

# Saving and Publishing Files to the Web

*In this lesson, you learn how to prepare worksheets for use on the World Wide Web. You also learn how to add hyperlinks to your Excel worksheets.*

## SAVING A WORKBOOK FOR THE WEB

You can save your Excel data to a Web site (or on your company's intranet) by converting your workbook to HTML format. When you save a workbook (or part of a workbook) in this way, it can be viewed through a Web browser.

**PLAIN ENGLISH**

> **HTML** Short for HyperText Markup Language, HTML is the language in which data is presented on the World Wide Web. To display your Excel data on the Web, you must convert it to this format.

You can save your Excel worksheets for the Web in different ways. You can save them in the HTML format so that they can be viewed but not changed: In this scenario, the data is considered *static*. However, you can update the data yourself as needed simply by *republishing* the workbook (we discuss this later in the lesson).

You also can save the worksheet (or the workbook) so that your data is *interactive*; this means that a user can view it and change it right in their Web browser. They also will see the results of any formulas or functions that you have placed in the worksheet as they add data to the interactive Web worksheet.

## CREATING AN FTP LOCATION

When you save your Excel workbook or worksheet for the Web, you can save the newly created HTML file directly to your Web site or to a location on your computer's hard drive. If you save the file to your hard drive, you can move it to the Web site later using Windows Explorer. If you are going to save the file directly to your Web site—or rather, to the Web server that hosts your Web site (on the Internet or your company's intranet)—you will need to create an FTP location. FTP stands for File Transfer Protocol, and it serves as a method of moving files from one computer to another (such as your Web server) on the Internet.

**PLAIN ENGLISH**

**FTP**    Short for File Transfer Protocol, FTP is used to move files from computer to computer on the Internet. Creating an FTP location on your computer enables you to save Web-ready content, such as Excel files, directly to your Web server.

Creating an FTP location enables you to save your Web-ready Excel files directly to the Web server that will host your Web site. To create an FTP location, follow these steps:

1. In Excel, select the **File** menu, and then select **Open**. The Open dialog box appears.

2. Click the **Save in** drop-down arrow at the top of the Open dialog box. Then, click **Add/Modify FTP Locations** on the drop-down list that appears. The Add/Modify FTP Locations dialog box appears (see Figure 20.1).

**FIGURE 20.1**
*The Add/Modify FTP Locations dialog box enables you to create an FTP location for your Web server.*

3. In the **Name of FTP Site** box at the top of the Add/Modify FTP Locations dialog box, type the name of the FTP site that coincides with your Web server. The FTP name for the Web server will be in the format `ftp.Web site name.com`. For example, if my Web site is `Habraken.com`, the correct FTP name would be `ftp.habraken.com`.

4. In the **Log on As** box, you must specify whether you log on to your Web server anonymously (Anonymous is the default) or whether a user name is required. Most Web sites hosted by an Internet service provider will require a user name and a password. Click the **User** option button, and then type the user name that you have been provided by your Internet service provider in the appropriate box.

5. If you specified a user name, click in the **Password** box and supply the password that is required for you to log on to your Web server (which is being specified as the FTP site).

6. Click the **Add** button to add the FTP location to the FTP sites list.

7. Click **OK** to close the Add/Modify FTP Locations dialog box.

8. You return to the Open dialog box. Click **Cancel** to close the Open dialog box.

Now that you have created an FTP location for your Web site, it will be available when you publish an Excel workbook or worksheet to your Web site. The next section discusses how to publish Excel content to a Web server.

## PUBLISHING AN EXCEL WORKSHEET TO THE WEB

After you have an FTP location setup that will allow you to save your Excel workbooks or worksheet to your Web server, you are ready to publish your Excel files to the Web. To publish your Excel worksheet (or the entire workbook), follow these steps:

1. If you're not publishing the entire workbook, select the cell range or item (such as a chart) that you want to publish.

2. Open the File menu and select **Save as Web Page**. The Save As dialog box appears, as shown in Figure 20.2. Notice that the Save As Type box says Web Page. This means that your worksheet will be saved in the HTML format.

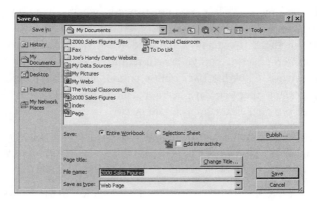

**FIGURE 20.2**
*Use the Save As dialog box to save your Excel worksheet for the Web.*

3. In the **Save in** list, select the FTP location that you created using the steps in the previous section (it will be at the very end of the list) or a folder on your hard drive where you want to save the HTML Excel file.

**TIP**

**Hey, Look Me Over!**—Before publishing your data, you might want to save it to a local hard drive first. You then can view it in your Web browser. If the file needs editing, you can reopen it in Excel and make any necessary changes, or you can use an HTML editor, such as Microsoft FrontPage, to make changes as needed. You then can publish the HTML file to its permanent location on your company's intranet or the Internet.

4. Perform either of the following:

   To save the entire workbook, select **Entire Workbook, Save** (skip the remaining steps.)

   To save a part of the workbook (such as a worksheet or a chart), choose **Selection**.

5. Type a name for the HTML file in the **File Name** text box.

6. To specify the title for the HTML file that will be created, click **Change Title** and change the title for the Web page in the Set Title dialog box (the title appears in the title bar of a user's Web browser when your page is viewed). After editing the title, click **OK** to close the Set Title box. Now you are ready to publish the Excel content.

7. Click **Publish**. The Publish as Web Page dialog box appears, as shown in Figure 20.3.

8. If you are not going to publish all the items on a particular worksheet or workbook, use the Choose list to select the item you want to publish.

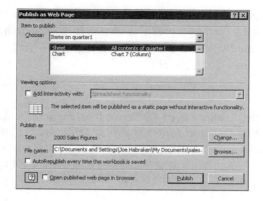

**FIGURE 20.3**
*The Publish as Web Page dialog box enables you to set options related to your Excel Web content.*

Before you leave the Publish as Web Page dialog box, you need to briefly learn about static versus interactive data, and then look at how you can have Excel data automatically updated to a Web page when you change the workbook or worksheet.

## STATIC VERSUS INTERACTIVE DATA

As you learned at the very beginning of this lesson, you can save your Excel data as static Web information or you can make it interactive, allowing users on the Web to input their own data and take advantage of the formulas and functions you have placed in the worksheet. If you want to place a snapshot of data, such as a quarterly report, onto the Web, you will want to publish static data. If you refer to Figure 20.3, you will notice that static data is the default.

To publish interactive data, where the information in the worksheet can be changed by a user viewing the worksheet using a Web browser, click the **Add Interactivity With** check box on the Publish as Web Page dialog box. Also, be sure that the drop-down list next to the check box displays **Spreadsheet Functionality**, which allows users to enter, update, copy, move, delete, format, sort, or filter data in a Web browser window (you will look at an interactive worksheet in a Web browser later in this lesson).

## COMPLETING THE PUBLISHING PROCESS

When you have determined whether the data will be static or interactive when published to the Web, you are ready to complete the Web publishing process. Follow these steps:

1. If you will be changing the contents of the Excel HTML file over time and want it automatically republished each time you save changes to the file, click the **AutoRepublish Every Time This Workbook Is Saved** check box. This will make it unnecessary for you to repeat the entire publishing process each time you change the contents of the Excel worksheet or workbook.

2. If you want, select the **Open Published Web Page in Browser** check box to launch your Web browser at the completion of the Web publishing process, so you can view the HTML file immediately.

3. When you have made all your selections in the Publish as Web Page dialog box, click **Publish**.

The Excel data will be published as an HTML file (Excel worksheets containing graphics and charts actually will be published as a group of files) to the location that you specified.

## VIEWING EXCEL DATA IN A WEB BROWSER

After you have published your Excel worksheet or workbook to a Web server (or a location on your computer's hard drive), you can view the data in any Web browser. Excel data that you publish as interactive data is best viewed in Internet Explorer (4.0 or better).

To view the Excel data, open your Web browser. Then, specify the Web site to which you published the Excel data in the Address box. Or, in the case of data that you published to your local hard drive, select **File, Open** in your browser window. In the Open dialog box that appears, type the location and name of the file, or use the Browse button to browse for the file. Click **OK** to close the Open dialog box and view the file.

Figure 20.4 shows static Excel data that has been published. As already mentioned, static data only supplies information; the data cannot be manipulated in the browser window.

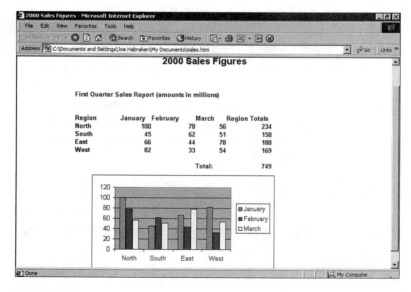

**FIGURE 20.4**
*Static data published for the Web.*

Excel workbooks or worksheets that have been published as interactive data actually can be manipulated within the browser window. This enables you to create worksheets that your clients can use on the Web. For example, you might create a worksheet that allows users to figure out how much a monthly car payment would be based on the car's principal (meaning the amount the car costs).

Figure 20.5 shows an interactive worksheet published to the Web. Users can input the price of a car and see what the monthly payment would be for a four-year loan at 8%.

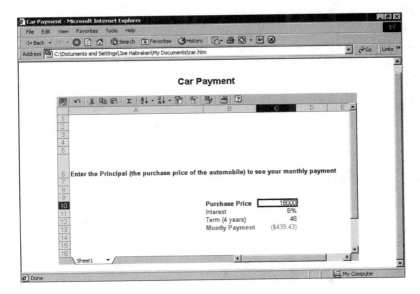

**FIGURE 20.5**
*Interactive data published for the Web.*

When you publish Excel data for use on the Web, you typically will want to incorporate the Web pages that you create into the series of other pages that are available on your Web site. This can be done using Web-page editing tools such as Microsoft FrontPage.

## ADDING HYPERLINKS TO A WORKSHEET

A *hyperlink* is a cell containing text (or values) or a picture that, when clicked, takes the user to a Web page, to a file on your hard disk, or to a file on a local network. Adding hyperlinks to Excel worksheets that you then publish to the Web makes it easy for users viewing your Web content to jump to other pages on your Web site.

Using hyperlinks in Excel worksheets that you do not publish for the Web enable you to quickly jump to another worksheet or workbook that contains information related to the Excel data that is currently being viewed in Excel. To add a hyperlink, follow these steps:

1. Select the cell (containing descriptive text or a value related to the file or location that will open when the hyperlink is clicked) or image you want to use for the hyperlink.

2. Click the **Insert Hyperlink** button on the Standard toolbar.

3. If asked, be sure you save your workbook. The Insert Hyperlink dialog box appears, as shown in Figure 20.6.

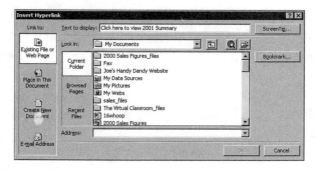

**FIGURE 20.6**
*Use the Insert Hyperlink dialog box to create a hyperlink in your Excel worksheet.*

4. Perform one of the following:

To link to a file or Web page, enter the address of the Web page or location of the file to which you want to link in the **Address** text box, or click **Browsed Pages** or **Recent Files** to select it from a list.

To link to a location within the workbook, click the **Place in This Document** button in the places bar. Then, enter the cell address in the **Type the Cell Reference** text box, or select it from the **Or Select a Place in This Document** list.

To create a link to a new workbook, click the **Create New Document** button in the places bar. Then, type a name for the document in the **Name of New Document** text box. To save the workbook in a directory other than the one shown, click the **Browse** button and select the directory you want to use.

To create a link to an e-mail address (so the link will open your e-mail program, display a message window, and automatically address the e-mail message), click the **E-Mail Address** button in the places bar. Then, type the e-mail address to which you want to link in the **E-Mail Address** text box, or select one from the **Recently Used E-Mail Addresses** list. If you want to enter a subject for the message, type one in the **Subject** text box.

5. To display a ScreenTip when the mouse pointer rests on the hyperlink, click **ScreenTip**, and enter the description you want to display. Click **OK**.

6. After you have made your selections in steps 4 and 5, click **OK** to close the dialog box. The text in the cell you selected becomes blue and underlined, meaning that it is now a hyperlink (images do not change color when they are used for hyperlinks).

When you move the mouse pointer over this link, it changes to a hand. Next to the hand, you can see the address of the link. Click the link, and you will jump to the appropriate worksheet, Web page, file, or e-mail program. The text of the link changes to purple to indicate that you have used the link.

If you need to change the text for a link later on, or to change the item to which the link points, right-click the link, and select **Hyperlink** from the shortcut menu. Then, select **Edit Hyperlink**. The Edit Hyperlink dialog box appears. Make your changes and click **OK**. To delete the link, right-click, select **Hyperlink**, and then select **Remove Link** from the shortcut menu.

In this lesson, you learned how to publish workbook files to the Web and how to add hyperlinks to your Excel worksheets.

# INDEX

# T

# U-V

# W-Z